My View From the Mountains

A Catskills Memoir

Patti Posner

Copyright © 2023 by Patti Posner

All rights reserved.

No part of this publication may be reproduced, distributed or transmitted in any form or by any means, including photocopying, recording, or other electronic or mechanical methods, without the prior written permission of the publisher, except as permitted by U.S. copyright law. For permission requests, contact:

HotelBrickman@gmail.com

For privacy reasons, some names, locations and dates may have been changed.

Book Cover by Patti Posner
Edited by Allen J. Sheinman
First edition 2023

Hotel Brickman Publishing
Weaverville, North Carolina

DEDICATION

My View from the Mountains is dedicated to my dad, Ben Posner.

And to all our guests and staff who had the time of their lives at the Hotel Brickman.

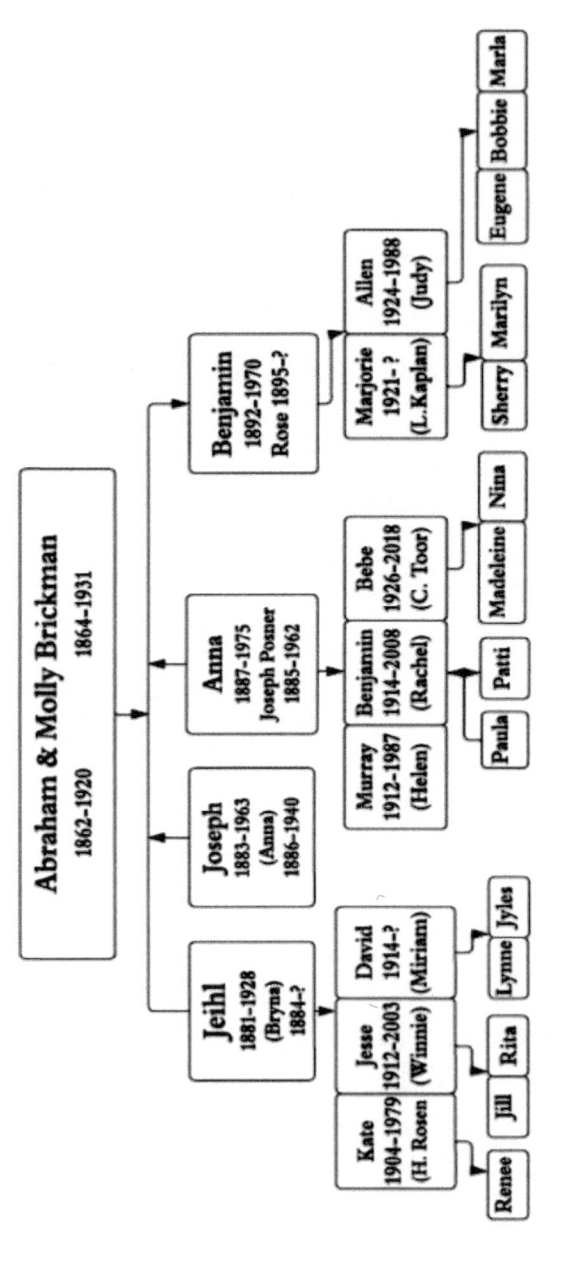

Standing: Anna and Jeihl Brickman
Seated: Molly, Ben and Abraham Brickman
In Russia

Contents

	Prologue: October 1997	1
1	The Rhythm of Hotel Life	3
2	Grandma's Story	6
3	The Brickman Begins, or A Family in Disarray	10
4	My Mother, Rachel Berson Posner	16
5	My Parents' Secret	22
6	The Seasons	28
7	Cast of Characters, Act I	34
8	My Uncle, His Wife and His Mistress	39
9	Cast of Characters, Act II	46
10	Two New Bellhops	49
11	Marriage # 1	53
12	My Second Marriage to a Bellhop	59
13	A Family Reunited	63
14	I Quit	67
15	Life at the Pink Table	72
16	Consequences	75
17	Matzoh Balls and Quaaludes	79
18	Breakfast: The Kitchen in Full Gear	85
19	Finding My Niche and My Voice	90
20	A Humbling Moment	96
21	Drama in the Dining Room	101
22	Life Between Meals	105
23	My Friend Jose	110

24	Jewish Roots	114
25	The Pearl	118
26	Uncle Murray Checks Out	123
27	Country Roads	130
	Epilogue	136
	Other Voices	138
	Acknowledgments	173

Prologue

October 1997

Memories come rushing in as I drive through South Fallsburg. I pass my old school, Fallsburg Elementary, now sadly boarded up and sagging with years of disuse. But, at least for now, the Pines Hotel remains open, a fraying string of buildings connecting to a storied tradition of hospitality that once saw as many as 500 resorts breathing life into the fabled Catskill Mountains. I drive by Skopps Bungalow Colony, a once busy summer family getaway now just a shadow of its former self. My heart begins to beat harder now; I'm getting nearer to the Brickman.

As I approach the driveway leading onto the grounds, I'm quickly reminded that this is no longer the hotel my family once owned. The Hotel Brickman sign has been removed, as have the tennis courts off to my left.

The stable still stands, though there is no sign (or smell) of horses. To the right is the Ranch House, a long motel-style building with 20 rooms (funny how I still remember the room count), but now lounge chairs no longer dot the lush green lawn with its two stone patios. The Ranch House had been my favorite of our various guest accommodations and the one I would have chosen had I been a guest and not the daughter of Ben Posner, one of the owners of the hotel.

And it's so quiet.

The buildings look the same but now serve as an ashram run by the SYDA Foundation, to whom we sold the Brickman at the end of 1986 after a long and eventful 74-year run. Instead of driving through to the main entrance and into the heart of the complex, I turn right, up the dirt road snaking behind the Ranch House to the back end of the property, the same route once taken by "bungalow people" who snuck in on foot. Many were inevitably discovered and asked to leave.

I drive by my former home, the one I shared with my second husband, then pass what had been the day camp where I spent my childhood years. Then I go down the hill toward the parking lot. I park just outside the back door to the kitchen. I try the door, which opens with the same creak of springs that began so many of my mornings, seemingly a lifetime ago.

The kitchen had been my domain for the last ten years of the hotel's existence, a noisy, bustling nexus of waiters coming and going, trays clattering, lots of shouting, all with the mission of feeding 600 ravenous guests three meals a day. I would orchestrate this mayhem from my station at a table the color of a pink flamingo, the air fragrant with pastrami and roast beef, Danish, and challah straight from the oven. Now the table is gone, and the vast space seems eerily hollow in the tranquil service of the ashram.

After I visit the kitchen, I walk over to the terraced area where our Olympic-sized outdoor pool once reigned as the focal point for our guest's busy day. But the grounds of what had been the Hotel Brickman have been transformed to reflect the austerity of the SYDA Foundation, and I am struck speechless: When my family owned the hotel, the terraces were lined with colorful chaise lounges: and now the terraces are empty. The pool has been filled in and turned into a lawn. Nothing feels familiar. I do not feel at home.

A few years later, I returned with my two cousins. As we approached the outdoor pool, a devotee of the ashram came up and asked us what we were doing there. We told him we were part of the Posner family that used to own this property, and we just wanted to look around. We were asked to leave, just like we used to tell the bungalow people.

The hotel was much more than the family business. It was my home, and I loved it. But on this day, I soaked up what vestiges of the past I could and moved on.

Chapter 1

The Rhythm of Hotel Life

My life in the Catskills had a steady rhythm. The hotel was either open or the hotel was closed. The rhythm defined how my life was structured. When the hotel was open, my life centered around the hotel, starting as a child in the day camp. As a teenager, I went into the teen group, where I began to notice all the cute waiters and busboys. And bellhops. My career started at the Brickman at the age of 15, first working at the front desk and then in the reservation office. By my mid-20s, I was managing the kitchen. When the hotel closed for the winter, my local friends and small-town life came into focus. I could easily switch from my hotel life to my life as a local. It was like finishing a good book just to pick up another.

My parents and I lived at the hotel during the "season," which was from the beginning of April through November during my teen years. The season was shorter when I was a kid, from Memorial Day Weekend to mid-September. As an adult, I had my own home on the premises and lived there year-round. When I was a child, our home was a two-room cottage behind the Ranch House. By my early teens, we had moved into an apartment in The Capital. Built in 1925, The Capital was the first of the Brickman's relentless building and expansion projects over the years, something all the competing hotels in the area did in a continuous effort to be ever-more modern.

The hotel was the dominant theme of my years living and working there. In many ways, it still influences my life to this day. As the Brickman recedes further into the past, the more those years make themselves known to me, allowing me to see how my Catskills experience created who I am today.

My life at the hotel seemed normal to me. I happily recall meals prepared by the hotel chef and shared with my grandmother, my dad and the butcher. All of us sitting around the pink-flamingo table in a kitchen the size of a warehouse, with soup pots large enough to swim in, skillets vast enough for a bath, and a dishwasher the size of a Sherman tank. It didn't seem unusual to me that we had menus printed daily from which to choose our meals, including eight choices each for lunch and dinner and more breakfast selections than could be found in most of the diners in the surrounding towns. I could go for a week and not eat the same dish twice. Or I could eat a kosher roast chicken every evening for dinner if I wanted to, and I sometimes did.

By now, you can tell that my childhood was not one of material deprivation. I did not grow up wondering where my family's next meal was coming from. I am an only child reared by overindulgent parents, each their own way. I can't tell you what a great cook I am or that I learned to cook by watching my mother create meals that sent delicious smells meandering up the long hallway leading to my bedroom. No, my mom spent many of her dinner hours in bed nibbling on cottage cheese while my dad took me out to dinner practically every night when the hotel was closed. During the summer, there was an entire kitchen staff to make my meals.

My mother, Rachel (Rae) Posner, was a troubled soul who was unable to serve as a proper role model for me. She suffered from crippling agoraphobia and spent much of her time alone in her room. She never got up with me in the morning during the school year to help me get ready for school. That was my dad's job. But she was always there to greet me after school (one of the pluses of her condition).

Ben Posner, my dad, was the one who bought my clothes, made my breakfast, drove me to school and took me out to eat most nights during the winter months. As I grew up in an era still marked by the traditional division of roles for men and women, what was expected of me was confusing. Since my mom relied on my dad and a maid to do the housework, I became unsure about what a woman's duties were supposed to be. My mom's inability and my dad's ease with accepting responsibility left me struggling to find a balance between the feminine and the masculine. Not surprisingly, I most often mirrored my dad's behavior, but it went beyond wanting to do things for myself or never asking for directions; it eventually extended to being a caregiver to troubled partners of my own.

And if that weren't enough, there was some old, foundational trouble in my family that no one ever discussed.

Chapter 2

Grandma's Story

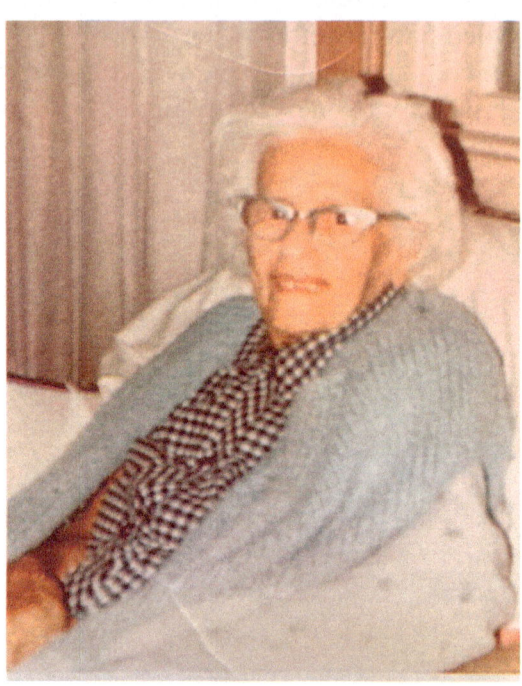

In June 1972, I was 22 and recently divorced, having completed three years and eight days (for those keeping score) of my first marriage. My high school friends were working toward their college degrees, and here I was, already a college dropout and divorcee. It was time to take stock and begin the process of finding myself. I also wanted to know the answer to a long-suppressed question: How come the place I called home, the Brickman Hotel, was almost devoid of Brickman relatives and loaded with Posners? It had long been a forbidden topic in the family.

One day that June, I found my courage and asked my grandmother, Anna Brickman Posner, if I could meet her in the kitchen after lunch. She was in her late 80s at this point and had her customary warm smile for me as we sat down at the pink-flamingo table. I told her I was very curious about our family and would love to know more about our family's history. Her face clouded over as she said in her thick Yiddish accent, "I do not know if I can open up that box." Then, seeing the disappointment on my face, she sighed and nodded in reluctant surrender. "I have not talked about all this in years," she said mournfully. "Parts of the story are so painful." Grandma didn't look at me as she began to bring up the past.

"To escape the violence in Russia, my family had to immigrate to America. Around 1902, my eldest brother, Jeihl, came alone to this county. After a year, he saved enough money to bring me and my brother Joseph to this country. I was 17." I couldn't picture my grandmother as a teenager. "And in 1904, my parents Abraham and Molly and my youngest brother Benjamin arrived. Ben was 12 at the time."

"Your brother Ben, that's Uncle Buzzie?" I asked, happy that I knew at least one of her brothers. She nodded yes as I smiled.

"My brothers, Jeihl and Joe, started a laundry on Madison Avenue and East 34th Street in Manhattan. We all went to work for them." This was the first time I had heard that Grandma had three brothers. I had assumed Ben was her only brother.

"My parents were in their early 40s when they came here. It was a big adjustment for them. My father hated working in the laundry. I found a job at Lord and Taylor," she said proudly as she shared this.

Grandma told me they all lived in her brother Jeihl's furnished one-bedroom, third-floor walk-up apartment on West 36th Street. Bryna and Jeihl slept in an alcove off the kitchen, Abraham and Molly slept in the only bedroom, while their children, Joseph, Annie and Benjamin, rolled out mats in the living room. They all shared a bathroom that was down the hall, a WOB — without bath, as we called it in the hotel business.

Cramped in their small apartment and bewildered by the fast pace of the city, Grandma told me her father had longed for the lush lawns and relative peace of the Russian countryside.

"Somehow, I don't remember how, my father heard of a Mr. Epstein who owned a farm in Swan Lake, New York. Mr. Epstein was looking for a partner. So my dad became a farmer again, partnering up with Mr. Epstein, and thus a few years after we came to this country, we moved to Swan Lake. I was single, so I had no choice but to go with them to the country. The farm had a big house and several barns, but the soil was so rocky it was impossible to plow. So they started to take in boarders, feeding them whatever food we produced on the farm."

Grandma stopped here for a moment, perhaps lost in thought. I heard her sigh, and then she continued. "At about the same time that all this was happening, your Posner grandfather, Joseph, also emigrated to the U.S. His original family name was Kuchdefrock, 'short coat' in Polish. His father had been a tailor. Grandpa's family changed their last name to Posner after the Polish town of Poznan, which he had traveled through as a young teen making his way, alone, to London to live with his older brother Morris, his wife, and their six daughters and one son. Morris was 18 years older than Grandpa and was well established in London when Grandpa arrived."

Both Posner brothers had left home while still in their teens, at their mother Beatrice's urging, because she wanted them to escape the abuse doled out by their father, Pincus, a deaf mute with an awful temper. When my grandfather, Joseph Posner, came to the U.S., he was already fluent in English, having lived for years in London.

All this was a revelation to me, including the news about another Posner brother. My Grandma explained: "Charlie was a horse thief and may never have left Poland. Grandpa never knew what happened to him. He would have been a young man during World War II. There is a good chance Charlie perished under the terror of Hitler. Grandpa rarely talked about him.

"Like my dad, your grandfather wanted to make a life for himself in the country. A Posner cousin, a friend of my parents, told Grandpa about our farm in Swan Lake. He checked in as a guest and checked out as a son-in-law." She giggled like a young girl as she told me this. "And that's how I met your grandpa. By the summer, we were engaged. "On January 1, 1911, we were wed in a joint ceremony with my brother Joseph and his new wife, Anna. Grandpa married the farmer's daughter," she joked.

"Joseph, T'Annie, as we called Anna, Jeihl and Bryna, remained in the city, working in the laundry. Benjamin went off to Cornell in Ithaca, New York, to study agriculture. He was the first in the family to graduate college," Grandma noted proudly. "When your mom came into the family and called her Aunt Annie, her Southern accent made it sound like "T'Annie." So we called her that. She loved it. This was great because there was so much confusion with our names." She smiled at the memory.

"The laundry was successful. The farm/boarding house was becoming profitable. However, my dad was having a hard time working with his partner Mr. Epstein. With a son-in-law to help run the aspiring boarding house, my father decided it was time to buy another property for them to run and grow.

"Not long after my marriage, my parents took a buggy ride to visit their friends, the Cohens, in South Fallsburg. They lived next door to what is now Skopps Bungalow Colony. While there, they walked over to the property next door, Pleasant Valley Farm House, and negotiated a deal to purchase the property for $3,500. The hotel kept that name until 1925 when it was incorporated and became the Brickman House Inc. or Hotel Brickman."

She opened her arms wide in a dramatic effect to punctuate her story. Now she was truly smiling. This was the woman I knew and loved, someone who used her sense of humor lovingly and often. She was friendly, well respected, spoke her mind freely, laughed easily and was extremely frugal.

"I have lots of Brickman documents. Come, I will show them to you." As we walked to her apartment, my excitement mounted. She took my hand like she did when I was a child. "Remember the games I used to play with you? Which room was where? I'd ask you where room 101 is, and by six years old, you could tell me which building 101 was in. I knew one day the hotel would be all yours." The thought of this was overwhelming and exhilarating, yet it made sense as my Uncle Murray had no children, and Ben's sister had no shares in the hotel.

Once we entered her apartment, she headed straight to the closet in the living room. "Sit," Grandma instructed me. She soon returned, carrying a large box. "I have all the documents that made the hotel ours. As you will see, my father bought the hotel from a woman, and even though I had three brothers, I ended up with the family business, and one day you, a woman, will be the hotel's owner."

More immediately, I would learn what caused the fracture in our family.

Chapter 3

The Brickman Begins, or A Family in Disarray

Back row, from left: Ben Brickman, Joseph Posner, Joe Brickman, Anna Brickman, Jeihl Brickman, Kate Rosen
Front row, from left: Murray Posner, Anna Brickman Posner, Abraham Brickman, Molly Brickman, Bryna Brickman, Jesse Brickman
Little boys in front: Ben Posner, David Brickman

The first document Grandma showed me was the original deed for the Hotel Brickman, dated May 2, 1912. My great-grandfather, Abraham Brickman, signed a contract to buy property consisting of "about 97 acres more or less." The seller, Matilda A. Richard, had inherited the land. The purchase price was $4000, which is approximately $125,000 today. The document reads as follows:

> This Indenture, made the tenth day of May in the year One Thousand Nine Hundred and Twelve (May 10, 1912) between

ABRAHAM BRICKMAN of 230 West 36th Street, New York City, party of the first part, and MATILDA A. RICKARD, STELLA M. HILL and GEORGE H. HILL, all of the town of Fallsburgh, Sullivan County, New York, parties of the second part, whereas, the said Abraham Brickman is justly indebted to the said parties of the second part in the sum of twenty-seven hundred (2700) dollars, lawful money of the United States, secured to be paid by their certain bond or obligation, bearing even date herewith, conditioned for the payment of the said sum of twenty-seven hundred (2700) dollars by the first day of September, Nineteen Hundred and Twenty-Four (September 1, 1924) on twenty-five hundred (2500) dollars and the interest thereon, to be computed from this date at the rate of six per centum per annum, and to be paid September 1, 1912, and annually thereafter.

Even though Abraham Brickman had possession of the property deed, it stated that "the seller and family may remain on premises until May 15 and are to have enough milk and eggs for family use." On November 15, 1919, Abraham Brickman hired Isaac Rodinsky, a local contractor, for the first of many steps in the expansion of the Brickman Hotel. Rodinsky was to build a three-story stucco building with two dining rooms, three other rooms, two rooms for toilets, one room for a shower and one for an office. The rest of the building would include 24 guest bedrooms and one summer kitchen. The price for all this came to $21,300 ($365,400 in today's money). The job was to be finished by June 25, 1920, just a few weeks before the July 4th weekend, the beginning of the summer season. The building would be known as The Capital.

"My dad, Abraham, died just months later, on September 26, 1920." I wish I had asked my grandmother how he died, but I didn't think to ask. His wife, Molly, and their four children now owned the hotel, which consisted of two buildings totaling 85 rooms, one barn, one shed and one stucco building with 25 rooms. The Brickman Hotel's value at his death was $35,000 (about $519,000 today).

Grandma continued her story as we scanned all the paperwork detailing the history. "Joseph, Jeihl and Bryna's laundry business began to falter in the early 1920s," she recalled. "Jeihl, now a part owner of the hotel, moved his family, which included their young sons, Jessie and Davie and their teenage daughter Kate, to South Fallsburg so that he and Bryna could live and work at the hotel."

Here she paused to reflect on her brother. "Jeihl was a good-looking man with a mustache and a small beard combed neatly on his oval face. He had a welcoming smile, and when I look at photos of him, I see Uncle Murray. Both with full heads of wavy hair and solid, captivating faces."

Good looks notwithstanding, integrating Jeihl and his family into the fabric of the hotel would prove an arduous process. Joseph (Grandma's brother) and his wife, Anna Brickman, remained in the city. Ben and his wife, Rose, were living in Minnesota.

By now, my grandparents, Joseph and Anna Posner, had two young sons, Murray, born in 1912, and Ben (my dad), in 1914. Jeihl and Bryna's sons were around the same ages, Jess born in 1911, and David, born in 1914. The four cousins shared a room at the hotel and attended a one-room schoolhouse just down the road.

"Your dad and uncle, 'the country boys' as we called them, now had to find ways to incorporate and include their city cousins, Davie and Jess, into their local and hotel life," Grandma continued.

"In the winter, as the rural roads were covered with snow and ice, the four cousins would get out their sleds and belly-flop down the steep hill leading to the front door of the schoolhouse. Your dad loved his life in the country and would get up early before going to school to milk the cows." Grandma smiled at the memory.

My dad had told me about the cows. He would describe the freshness of the milk and how he would squirt milk into his mouth directly from the cows' udders. Years later, while holding an egg in his hand, he fondly described how he'd catch an egg from under a chicken, stick a pin in the top of the egg and suck out the yolk. My response, "Yuck!"

Grandma and I spent the rest of the afternoon going through all the other papers, pictures, deeds, receipts, contracts and certificates. She looked exhausted, but when I asked her if she wanted to continue this another time, she said no. And so she went on. "Murray and Dad had always been 'the boys' but now, with Jess and Davie around, 'the boys' also included them. The close living quarters, and perhaps the closeness of their ages and similarities in their personalities, made their relationship more antagonistic than affectionate. My sons and

Jeihl's sons struggled to find their place in the hotel. Meanwhile, our boarding house was transforming into a resort. Life was busy, communal and contentious. I found myself on edge all the time."

She paused again, lost in thought. The ghosts of the past seemed to be catching up with her. After a few minutes, she went on. "A few years after Jeihl moved to the hotel, in June of 1928, just as we were beginning to figure out the family hierarchy and roles for the boys, your grandpa and Jeihl were in a car accident. The hotel chauffeur was driving, Jeihl was in the front passenger seat and Grandpa was in the rear seat next to a guest." Her eyes filled up with tears. I got up to get her a glass of water. She took a sip and went on with her story.

"Without warning, the car careened off the road into a telephone pole just where Route 42 sweeps out of town. Grandpa spent over a week in the hospital. The driver and the guest were not hurt. My brother was killed instantaneously." Tears streamed down her cheeks. I just sat there, not knowing what to do or say.

After a while, she was able to continue. "Bryna, now a widow, found herself living alone amongst her in-laws. With me. She had always been a complicated woman. We never got along. I cannot say I liked her. Contentions escalated after Jeihl's death. Whatever relationship I had with Bryna was *nisht* good.

"My mother, Molly Brickman, was now the family's matriarch. She had an endearing smile, much like yours, Patti. Although she tried hard to keep the family intact, she could not achieve this. She died during the summer of 1931, just three years after Jeihl, her son. The shares in the hotel were left to me, Grandpa, my two brothers and Bryna. Tensions had been flaring since my father's death, tempers escalated after my brother died. With my mother dead, the stress on the family was too much. We were a family in disarray."

Years later, after I was reunited with my Brickman family, Jess's daughter, Rita Brickman Domnitz, shared with me what she knew of our story. I learned that during our family unraveling, Jess Brickman was working as an accountant in the city, having recently graduated from New York University. Davie was also living in New York. Bryna was basically alone and isolated at the hotel. She often complained to Jess that the Posners were not treating her well and that she was miserable. This prompted Jess to come home to help his mother deal with the family. While Bryna struggled to find her place in the hotel, unbeknownst to Bryna and her sons, Grandpa was looking for ways to buy her out of the business.

My Grandma looked shaken as she relived her memories. She took a breath and continued. "The final break occurred one fateful morning during the summer of 1937 when Jess punched Grandpa on the hotel's front porch. And that was it. The family was unable to recover. Your Uncle Murray had just earned his law degree," she continued, smiling as she said law degree. "He was central in the negotiations that led to the unwinding of the family. Bryna thought Murray was dishonest throughout the transactions. He was not. What Bryna did not know was that Grandpa had created a separate company, The Joseph Posner Company, which bought Joseph, my brother, and Benjamin and Rose Brickman's shares of the hotel."

Grandma handed me the paperwork from the Joseph Posner Co. I wanted to read it, but my grandmother was by now freely sharing this story with me, and I didn't want to do anything to impede her flow.

"Throughout 1938, there was so much tension in the family. It was so stressful for all of us. The Joseph Posner Co., though, was able to buy out Bryna that year. The following year, 1939, we bought out Ben and Rose. Because Ben had a profession outside of the hotel, the sale was amicable. Which is why we were still so close." She stopped for a moment to collect her thoughts.

Years later, my dad told me that after they bought out Bryna in '38, the Brickman was a small hotel deep in debt. He recalled they made about $59,000 for the whole summer season. The hotel began its true expansion after World War II. They built several buildings adding over 200 guest rooms, including the Ranch House in 1949 and the Villas. In 1955, they built the outdoor pool with all its terraces, and a few years after, they built the indoor pool, tennis courts, the bridge and the nightclub. By the time we sold the hotel, we had just over 300 guest rooms and close to 100 rooms for our staff.

"My sister-in-law, T'Annie, died in 1940," Grandma continued. "She was only 53. Her husband, my brother Joseph, was still a partner in the hotel, but he left the running of it to Grandpa and me and your dad and Murray. We were all very friendly.

"By the time the war ended, Joseph was dating quite a few women. We were concerned that things could become contentious if he remarried. Grandpa and I had had enough of dealing with sisters-in-law, so we asked him to sell us his shares of the hotel. We offered him the same deal we had with my brother Ben. We never realized that buying him out would be as difficult as it was with Bryna.

"Finally, in December of 1946, Joseph agreed to sell his shares of the hotel to your dad and Uncle Murray. They made payments to him for years until the $61,000 they owed him was paid off. Now our sons were our partners in the hotel. After the papers were signed, I never saw my brother again." Here she stopped for a moment before finishing her story.

"I inherited Grandpa's shares after he died in August of 1962. It wasn't until 1968 that I passed all my shares to my sons. And that's when they became the sole owners of the hotel.

"Those years of family tension were the hardest years of my life. The hotel was our savior when my family came to this country. We created a life for ourselves here, a sanctuary for us, and the many Jews who were our guests. But it was the destroyer of the Brickman family." She wiped away her tears and was quiet for a long time.

Even as Grandma seemed to be coming undone by her telling me of our history, I began to feel complete. The name Brickman surrounded me my whole life and felt more like my name than Posner. I forever seemed to be known as "Patti-from-the-Brickman." But I had always felt an emptiness knowing that there was a history being kept from me. And now I knew.

By 1946, the Posners were the sole owners of the Brickman Hotel. They owned a resort deep in debt yet full of potential. When all the exhausting negotiations were finalized, my grandfather semi-retired and left the hotel's daily operations to his sons. Murray was 34 and my dad was 32. Grandpa asked only that he and Grandma have a place to live on the grounds and to keep their salaries. Grandma stayed active in the hotel her whole life, never giving up her post in the kitchen.

My grandfather followed his passions by sitting on the boards of The Monticello Hospital and the Associated Mutual Insurance Co. which he helped found in 1913, along with other Jewish hotelmen who were rejected from insuring their hotels by established insurance companies.

The Posner boys, Murray and Ben, were in business.

Chapter 4

My Mother, Rachel Berson Posner

I often wonder what it would have been like to have had a mother who didn't shield her life in a lie. I imagine us sitting on the porch of the cottage behind the Ranch House. She tells me she wants to share something with me. As she begins, she touches my arm, gazing at me, looking for forgiveness. And just as I imagine the first words of her confession, the scene fades. And once again, I am alone.

My mother's parents, Michael and Ida Berson, immigrated to the U.S. in 1908. They fled Lithuania at a time when it was a perilous place for Jews. They found their way to Portsmouth, Virginia, where my grandfather went to work for his brother Aaron, who owned a dress shop — Berson Brothers Ready to Wear and Millinery. Portsmouth was where my mother first learned to sing in the neighboring black churches, sitting in the back "with all the little colored kids," she told me more than once, her Southern accent springing to life in recalling this happy time.

"After church, all the little colored kids and me, we'd all go to the train tracks, the elevated ones, on the edge of town," she would recall. "Some of us would climb onto the tracks. I'd catch a whopping when my mother found out. She didn't like me playing on the tracks, and she didn't want me hanging out with the Negroes, either. But oh, their music, how I love the music." And here, she would put her right hand on her heart as if it were a pledge. Then she would sing "Amazing Grace" in a clear, lilting voice, and I felt protected for those few moments when she must have felt the grace of the song rekindling sparks within her.

My mother managed her adult world by incrementally retreating into the privacy of her home, where her fears and self-deception grew so thick that by the time I was born, there was no way to penetrate the wall she had built to protect herself.

Every morning my mother made herself a cup of Sanka with a bit of milk. Then, with her cup and saucer in hand, she'd walk up the long hallway to her bedroom, droplets of coffee landing on the white linoleum flooring, forming a trail. If I heard her humming "Ac-cent-tchu-ate the Positive," an old Andrew Sisters song, I'd smile because I knew it might be an okay day.

She'd place the coffee cup on her French provincial nightstand. Propping herself against her pillows, she'd pull the covers over her chest. Then she'd light up a Parliament and pick up the phone for her morning chat with her sister Shirley. Her day had begun.

On one of these mornings, I heard my mother talking to Shirley about a doctor she had once known. I was coming into her room to ask her something. I stopped when I heard her talking to her sister. I hung just out of sight by her bedroom door to eavesdrop, something I often did when she chatted with her sister, hoping to discover a few more precious pieces of her life that she so carefully hid from so many — most of all me. I used to wish she would notice me standing there eavesdropping, hoping that if she did, she would share her story with me.

"You remember how hard it was for me after he broke our engagement?" I heard my mother say. Now *that* was news.

It took me years to piece together the backstory of my mother's life. I had to become a detective, talking to family members and, of course, eavesdropping to uncover faint traces of her life that had rippling effects on both of us. I wish we could have had a relationship that allowed us to talk freely to each other, mother and daughter, so that she could have shared her life with me, helped me to understand her, and, in the process, better come to know myself. But that proved impossible. Barricading herself in her bedroom, she left me alone, feeling more neglect from her than love.

After hearing about her engagement, I returned to my room and sat on my bed for a long time. I didn't know how to process this information; I was only 12 or 13 at the time. At that moment, though, I learned that before my mom met my dad, she was engaged to Malcolm Bergman, a surgeon. She called him Doc.

Over the next few weeks, I heard my mother talk to my aunt several times about Malcolm. As I stood just outside her bedroom door, I listened as she rehashed the story with her sister, who, of course, already knew the story's details. Shirley, at the time, was living in Richmond, Va., and was newly married to her husband, Sam Perlstein.

One morning I heard my mom say to Shirley, "I had gone to the shop early that morning. It was a Friday, and Mumma stayed home to make dinner. I was unpacking boxes of new dresses when I heard the door to the shop open. Doc called out to me. I was surprised — I thought he was at the hospital. It was barely 9 a.m. He sat on the sofa in the middle of the store and motioned for me to sit next to him. And that's when he said, 'I cannot marry you. I've met someone else.' Doc looked at me for a moment as if I were a stranger. Then he got up and walked out. I haven't heard about him in all these years. Until just now, Shirley."

My mother was devastated by his rejection. As she told her sister, she closed the shop and ran home. She stood on the front stoop of their home for several minutes before entering, attempting to compose herself. She didn't want her parents to know she had been crying, but she couldn't hide her pain.

As my mother stepped into the kitchen, her mother asked her what was wrong. "Mumma, it's over! Doc called off our engagement! He found someone else!" she cried. Instead of comforting her daughter, my grandmother blurted out, "You'll end up an old maid!" Then she ran out of the kitchen as if it were her own engagement that had just been broken.

A few minutes later, my grandfather entered the living room and saw my mother crying on the couch. My mom looked up at him, but he turned away without saying a word and walked down the hall to his bedroom. I wonder if she felt more neglect than love, the same I did.

The last time I overheard my aunt and mother discussing Malcolm, I heard an unfamiliar lilt in my mother's voice. She was telling Shirley that their brother Julius was the one who showed her the most compassion. She told Shirley about how he held her until she stopped crying. Then I heard them laughing about how my mom and Julius had to share a bedroom. Even though my mother loved her brother, not getting married meant they would have to keep sharing a bedroom. She had counted on her marriage to Malcolm to release her from that arrangement.

After Doc left the picture, my mother stayed in bed for a long time, a preview of a habit that would become more pronounced over the years. Julius would bring her meals and share town gossip, news from the bank where he worked and updates on baseball, the siblings' shared passion. My grandmother started nagging her to go up to New York to do some buying for the store. Julius agreed with their mom that a shopping trip would do her good. She had enjoyed them in the past. He also suggested she might enjoy a vacation at one of the hotels springing up in the Catskills. He joked with her, "You might meet a nice Jewish boy." A vacation didn't appeal to her at first but she soon warmed to the idea of getting away from the depressing scene at home.

With Julius' encouragement, she sent in a deposit to the Brickman Hotel for a week's vacation in July of 1935. A week later, she received a handwritten confirmation from the owner's son, Ben Posner. "I'll pick you up at the train station in South Fallsburg," he wrote. "His handwriting was large and legible," she recalled, "and I took it to mean this man had character." It would turn out that the note from Ben Posner was standard issue to all guests arriving by train, but her interest was already piqued.

First, she took the train to New York City, and by the time she arrived, the gloom of the past few months had begun to evaporate. "My days were full," she remembered. "I went from one wholesaler to another, looking at dresses, designs and my favorites, furs and shoes, for the store." It was a warm summer morning when, with the work part of her trip done, she headed across the Hudson River to Weehawken, New Jersey, to catch the O & W train (the New York, Ontario and Western Railroad) to South Fallsburg. Unfortunately, this was all I could find out about from my mom's side of the family.

Fortunately, my father was able to pick up the story. Every weekday and twice on Sundays, he met the O&W as it pulled into

South Fallsburg, driving past the lush green woods with towering evergreens that lined the country roads on the short trip from the hotel to town. On this July afternoon, he arrived at the station just as a striking young woman descended the train's steps. She wore a black fitted dress with matching gloves, her size-5 polka-dot pumps and a stylish turban hat completing her outfit. She looked a little like Liz Taylor and sauntered like Judy Garland. And she knew it.

My father got out of his car, held up a sign saying "Hotel Brickman" and watched as the woman approached him. "Going to the Brickman?" he asked. She replied affirmatively, and he detected a Southern accent. "My parents own the hotel," he said, suddenly wanting to impress her. He took her bags and asked her to sit up front with him. They made small talk on the 15-minute drive to the Brickman, and then he escorted her into the lobby.

That night, as he stepped into the dimly lit nightclub, he saw her alone at the bar. She wore a red strapless dress, with a satin shawl draped over one arm. The bartender had placed a Manhattan in front of her. She didn't notice him at first. My father was partially hidden behind a cluster of people. He tapped a full pack of Camels on the wall beside him and pulled out a cigarette. As he filled his lungs, their eyes locked. He was young and handsome. His dark brown eyes gave him a mysterious and alluring look. He walked up to her at the bar and ordered a Scotch. They chatted while sipping their drinks. Then he took her hand to lead her to the dance floor. They mamboed and tangoed until dawn.

Over the following week, Ben and Rae spent every evening together. They met at the bar for drinks each night before the show started, and after the show they took long romantic walks around the hotel, sharing their stories. Though they had just met, my dad thought he already knew all he needed to know about this attractive young Southerner.

On Saturday night, her last night at the hotel, my mother was once again sitting at the bar. She had on a tight black dress. Her Manhattan was in front of her as my dad sat down. Looking at one another, they knew this was their last night together. "Rae, let's get out of here." He took her hand and they walked out of the nightclub. They sat on swings on the rambling lawn outside the Main Building. Finally, he found the courage to ask her, "Rae, can you come back for the Labor Day weekend?" She looked at him and said, "I'd love to, precious Benny," her soft drawl caressing him.

Two years later, in 1937, my parents drove up to the Town Hall in a big black Buick. As they filled out their marriage licenses, my dad casually asked my mother, "How old are you?" A simple question, but my mother struggled for a moment, took a deep breath, and said simply, "We are the same age." With this wiping out of six years, to be once again 23, her lie became invisible on center stage.

My mother's answer might not seem so momentous, but it proved to be the first brick of the wall she built to protect herself. A wall without an entrance for her only living child. Over the course of my childhood years, she managed her world by retreating into the privacy of her home. Her limitations melted into normal, so that it seemed natural for her to spend days in bed, to see her husband and daughter go out for dinner most nights while she stayed home. She could drive up to 30 miles from home until I was about 13, but eventually, that was too much for her. Finally, it became difficult for her to venture further than her front porch. There she would hold court for visits from friends or staff.

Chapter 5

My Parents' Secret

June 6, 1937

At least twice a week, I share a meal with my daughter, Jo Anna. On these occasions, I'm often startled by her honesty; our laughter brings me joy, our love is palpable. I look at her and think: What does it feel like to sit with your mother, have a delicious meal and enjoy a funny conversation? What does it mean to be able to see your mother's love? I also wonder how it feels for her to fight with me, both of us expressing our pain and fear, thrashing out our problems until we inevitably regroup in each other's arms, knowing that this latest clash will only help us grow closer. What does it feel like to know your mother will do what it takes to be a loving mother? A mother who will show up no matter what?

    As a teenager, when I'd come home from high school, I often heard my mother's soulful singing, piercing our home's loneliness. If she didn't call out to me when I came home, I would softly step into the kitchen to give her a few extra moments of privacy. Mahalia

Jackson would be wailing on the record player in the den, and my mom would sing along with her. I loved those moments when I heard the mournful crooning of my mother.

After getting a snack, I'd tiptoe up the carpeted hallway and watch her swaying to the pounding beat of the old Negro gospels. Sometimes in those lingering minutes, she'd sing my favorite: *Amazing grace, how sweet the sound.* Then, when she noticed me, she'd stop singing and turn away to dry the tears flowing freely down her cheeks. Did singing help to ease the burdens she carried? I hoped so.

"You know, I used to sing on stage," she often told me after she dried her tears. I found this hard to believe. I'd seen photos of her on stage at the hotel in the early days when she was so young, poised and confident. She'd be standing in the middle of the stage in the hotel's casino, a mic in her hand. I could almost hear her singing "September Song": *"And these few precious days, I'll spend with you..."* I longed to know this singer, the woman who stood behind the mic, but that person had exited the stage before I was born.

Most mornings, my mother slept in. On weekends, when she finally left the comfort of her bed, she'd come and find me lying on the couch in the den watching Saturday-morning TV. "Did you have breakfast yet?" she'd ask. Her breath was slightly stale, and I would turn my head away from her as she bent over to kiss me. "Ma, brush your teeth first," I'd say. The thin lace strap of her pink satin nightgown was about to slide off her left shoulder, and the outline of her heavy breasts showed through her nightgown, causing me to look away. "I must have a cigarette and a cup of coffee," she'd say and walk away, ignoring my crack about her breath and forgetting whether I had eaten breakfast.

My mom may have tried to mother me when I was a child, but when I look back at old black-and-white photos, it feels as if I am merely a prop. One image is incredibly vivid: I am two years old. My mother is making an entrance from the front door of our home. The camera catches her as she steps onto the driveway. She is pushing me in a stroller. I am dressed in an adorable outfit, all bows and lace. mother is glancing forward, knowing the camera is upon her. She smiles fittingly, and there I am, in my stroller, a backdrop to my mother.

Though she spent most of her time at home, she loved clothes and had the wardrobe of a woman who still sang and danced on the hotel's stage. Her closet was adorned with satins and silks in vibrant oranges and reds. I knew from the old photos and family stories that she once had enjoyed being the focus of attention. Sometimes I would stare into those shots of her on stage in a gorgeous tight-fitting dress, elegant on her feet. I'd stare, but all I could conjure up was the woman who lay in bed most of my life.

Just as the satins and silks my mother wore were adornments, the clothes she picked for me when I was very young made me feel like a fashion doll rather than a kid getting ready to romp around a day camp. When the weather turned cold, she liked to dress me in a camel-hair peacoat with matching leggings. I felt uncomfortable in most of the clothes she picked out for me. They were always too formal and stylish. They didn't provide the warmth I yearned for from my mother.

Often she would brush my brown curly hair, which was about as physically close to me as she could comfortably get. Whenever her eyes wandered over my face, she'd invariably stop on my nose. While my mother had a cute little button nose that complemented the beauty of her face, mine was enormous, longer than my index finger, and could give Jimmy Durante a run for his money. She would take her finger and attempt to scrunch the tip of my nose; maybe she thought if she did this enough times, she'd create the desired appendage for her only child.

When I was 10, in 5th grade, my friends and I were on the school playground. They were talking about their brothers and sisters. Being an only child, I felt out of place, so I blurted out, "I like being an only child." Everyone knew this, of course, we had all been together since kindergarten, but it just came out.

Cliffy, one of my classmates, turned to me with this strange expression on his face. I don't think he said this to be mean, but he said, "No, you're not. Your parents had a baby before you." There, it was out, splashing around in the mud on the playground. I wanted to pick up those words and shove them down his throat. "That's not true," I screamed. "Yes, it is. I heard my parents talking to the Newburgs about the baby your parents had when Mrs. Newburg was pregnant with Marvin."

My dad picked me up after school, as he did every day. Usually, we went to town and sat at the counter in Gold's Pharmacy, drinking egg creams. I loved spinning on the red plastic-covered stools. But today was spinning out of control. As my dad reached over to open the door, I said, "Let's go home." He looked perplexed. "No egg creams? Are you feeling okay, honey?" He touched my forehead. I still couldn't talk.

We headed out of the parking lot of my elementary school. When he made the left at the traffic light, I knew he was taking me home. My mother greeted us at the front door; she had been making herself a cup of Sanka in the kitchen. Before I even put down my book bag, I screamed at them: "How could you not tell me? There was a baby before me!"

"How did you find out?" my parents said in unison. "Yes, we had a daughter," my mom confirmed, "Paula Ellen, who died a year before you were born." After she revealed her name, she quickly picked up her instant coffee and returned to bed. My dad looked at me, tears flowing down his cheeks, took me in his arms and said, "I am so sorry we didn't tell you."

My mother and I never talked about Paula again. But, years later, I found a photo of Paula when she was only two months old. There is a note on the back, written by my mother to her mother, *"Mumma, look how cute her nose is. Isn't she beautiful?"* Was it possible that when my mother tried to shorten my nose, she was looking to feel the presence of Paula?

During the first few months of my own daughter's life, I noticed that my dad was nervous around Jo Anna. He'd look at her with such love, longing and hesitation. Now that I was a mother, their loss became more tangible as I watched my mother sing lullabies to her only granddaughter. The more I held my daughter in my arms, I knew I needed to finally know the story of Paula's short life.

One evening while my dad was holding Jo Anna, I again noticed his apprehensiveness. I told him, "Dad, she's not going to die as Paula did." He looked up at me with such sadness. And then he shared with me, "The first time I held you, I thought you were going to die." I was motionless, trying to absorb my father's words. "And now you're 27 and a mother yourself."

A few weeks later, he took me out for dinner, just the two of us, as he had done throughout my childhood. After we ordered, my dad told me now that I was a mother, he needed to share what he could about other pregnancies they had before I was born.

"After I came home from the Army in 1945", he said, "Mom and I were already married eight years and eager to start a family. I was called up to serve in the army. 1941. I was sent overseas, leaving Mom at the hotel. I knew my parents would look after her.

"After a while, Mom decided to go to Portsmouth and live with her parents. She thought she'd feel more at home with her family. When that didn't work out, she went to live with Aunt Shirley. Your cousin Bob was just a kid, and his brother Norman had a dreadful disease.

"In the years before the war, we were enjoying ourselves at the hotel, Mom was adjusting to small-town life, and we were getting to know one another. We wanted to start a family. But unfortunately, that didn't happen as easily as we had hoped. We had two miscarriages and one stillborn baby." He was fiddling with a packet of sugar as he told me this.

"And then, on March 26, 1949, Paula was born. Mom held on to Paula so fiercely when the doctor first handed her to your mother. She was our first baby to survive." I lowered my head, fighting back tears as my dad spoke. We were so happy and relieved. And then Paula died just three months later." He took a deep breath, wiped his tears and continued. "When I held you for the first time, all I could think about was Paula. I felt the same way when I first held Jo Anna all these years later."

And then he stopped talking. I waited as my father gathered his thoughts. I felt uncomfortable listening to this story, but I needed to know. I was so grateful to him for sharing this with me.

Finally, he continued, "It was June, and the hotel was open. So I left the house early that morning. A few hours later, the switchboard operator got a hysterical call from Mom. The operator handed the phone to me. All I remember was Mom screaming into the phone, 'Paula is dead.' I don't know how I got home.

"When I walked into the house, I found Mom sitting next to the crib, singing a lullaby to our baby. She said the house had been quiet when she woke up that morning. So she rolled over and fell back to sleep for another hour. A real luxury with a three-month-old baby." Then the awful discovery.

As my dad was talking, I realized then that Paula must have died in what was to become my bedroom. "Mom wasn't able to go to the funeral; she was so distraught. I felt paralyzed." My dad looked up at me and smiled as he continued. "Then, five months later, we found out

Mom was pregnant again. It was then that I decided never to be unhappy again. But your mom collapsed into her sorrow."

Finding out about Paula was the first moment of numbness in my life. It was hard to absorb that I had not been my parent's only child and that they had not shared this with me. I cannot imagine the mixture of emotions that must have swirled within both of them, grieving and expecting another baby, all at the same time.

"And 14 months later, on May 27, there you were," my dad said, smiling. "I remember looking down at you in disbelief and wonder — a healthy newborn in my arms."

Chapter 6

The Seasons

My life was defined by the seasons of the hotel. July and August were "the season," when the Brickman hosted throngs of New Yorkers on their yearly getaways to the country. As a child, I was a camper in the day camp. Then I graduated to the teen group, which is when I began to notice all the cute waiters. And bellhops. My career officially began in 1965, when I started working in the office; I was 15. By my mid-20s, I was managing the kitchen.

The spring and fall were technically the "off-season," when Monday through Friday, we hosted senior-citizen groups, and on weekends, conventions as diverse as Jewish community centers, Gamblers Anonymous, and weekends devoted to Polka bands and dancing. Then there were the religious seasons, Passover welcoming in spring and Rosh Hashanah, the Jewish New Year, ushering in fall.

Labor Day marked the end of summer for the "city folk" and those of us fortunate to call South Fallsburg home. The day before, South Fallsburg was a bustling tourist town, while the day after, it suddenly was back to being a small rural community of predominantly Jewish families. Gone were the waiters and busboys, their white shirts spattered with yesterday's meals, their bowties hanging provocatively as if to signal, "Off duty, I'm on the prowl." Gone were the counselors in their frayed jeans and the cocktail waitresses in their short skirts, suggesting to the waiters and busboys, "Come and get me." Gone were the bellhops, musicians and comics, coffee shop staff and lifeguards. As soon as the vacationers and summer staff left, the small-town atmosphere of South Fallsburg returned, like a foam pillow remembering its form. South Fallsburg was home again.

I loved when the bustle of summer halted and the pace of my life changed. As a child, Labor Day signaled the start of the school year, and I looked forward to seeing my friends. As a teenager, the day was bittersweet, the lure of my local friends calling me home even as my summer love returned to the city. I savored the sadness for days. On Labor Day, 1977, I was a new mom, cradling my daughter. As a young married woman, I felt a sense of peace; time for my husband and daughter, time for myself and time for friends. The day after Labor Day felt like the town was ready to embrace the fall and await the quiet of winter.

Just after Labor Day, our town took on a soft autumn chill and contracted back to a small rural enclave of 1,200 primarily Jewish people who resumed greeting each other by name as they strolled down a markedly quieter Main Street. Within weeks after Labor Day, the local foliage magically transformed into sumptuous salutations of fall. Ambers, rusts and dazzling reds dressed our country roads, and once again I'd be in awe of nature's cycle, another sign confirming the continuity and depth of living in a small town. I loved walking down Main Street, nodding to acquaintances and stopping to talk to friends. Local eyes were always wandering, knowing they would alight on someone they knew.

Many locals made their living from the "city folk," including doctors, plumbers, restaurateurs, bungalow-colony owners, butchers and laundromat operators. The start of fall was a time for the store owners to slow down and enjoy catching up with loyal customers. At 10 a.m., locals could be found at the post office parking lot, knowing that many of their friends would greet them there. The post office bustled with conversation and catch-ups. "How was your summer?" "Over," the rhythmic response. It was community life at its best, warm and nurturing.

All these years later I can recall a typical off-season day in town that began when I visited the post office. As I bent down to open the hotel's mailbox, Mrs. Roffman came over to say hello. Mr. and Mrs. Roffman, as everyone in town knew them, owned Roffman's Candy

Store. Their store had a front stoop, and when walking in I was always bowled over by the amount of merchandise they crammed into the store. I imagined the Roffmans receiving their merchandise and then hurling it onto the shelves. If some fell to the floor, it just added to the ambiance. I said goodbye to Mrs. Roffman and walked back to Main Street.

When I walked the few short blocks from the Post Office to Malman's Hardware Store, I knew almost everyone I passed. I couldn't resist poking my head into Frank and Bob's Delicatessen, where most mornings, local politicians, hotel owners, shopkeepers, plumbers and electricians met for watered-down coffee and fresh Kaiser rolls. The dark paneled walls were lined with photos of entertainers like Buddy Hacket, Milton Berle and others whose careers had largely begun in the mountains and who had dropped in on a hot summer night for pastrami on rye or a fatty corned beef sandwich.

I loved hearing the heated conversations bellowing from table to table. Views varied, arguments ranged from local topics to the Cold War to the young State of Israel. Democrat and Republican friends came so close to one another that spittle bounced between them. What tied these men together was not their political viewpoints, not their sense of community, but the lingering aroma of pastrami that planted itself on winter jackets. It was hard to hide in our town.

The front window of Malman's Hardware was a haphazard display of kitchen gadgets and handyman tools. Before I walked in, I knew a waft of cigar smoke would hit me, signaling that a poker game was taking place behind the cash register. The players, all prominent Fallsburg men, were chewing on their long cigars while playing five-card stud. Murray "Moose" Malman presided over the table as usual. When he saw me, Moose got up from the table and went over to the counter to retrieve the order my father had called in.

I smiled to myself. My dad knew I hadn't mastered the language of hardware and called to ensure I got the right size nails.

When "Moose's" wife, Bea, thought he had lost enough for the day, she'd holler down from their upstairs apartment to end the game. As her voice echoed from the stairs, the poker players folded their cards, and squished their cigars. The game was over.

With my small brown bag of nails, I crossed the street to Pop-Ins Restaurant. My good friend, Audrey, was waiting at our table by the corner window. As I walked in, I noticed my mother's friends having coffee. They wanted me to join them, but when I pointed to Audrey, they understood that Audrey and I had a lot to discuss. We didn't see each other much when The Brickman was open.

Helen Kaufman, the owner of Trudy's, the toy store across the street, was standing at the counter and ordering something to go. She looked at me, her smile saying, "The summer must be over if you're at Pop-Ins this early." She was dressed in one of her trademark cheerless house dresses that make her look shorter than she was, her dark masculine shoes adding to her frumpy look. But her toy store was colorful, like a cascade of lollipops.

The Pauls were at another table. They owned the furniture store in town. I waved hello, but they were engrossed in conversation and did not see me. I didn't intrude, but I was curious; they looked as if they had just captured a juicy piece of gossip. As in any small town, gossip was a pastime of many of our locals, often tossed around haphazardly. The intricate lives of most of our neighbors could be splayed on Main Street if their behavior strayed too far from what was considered appropriate. Gossip, another thread in our connection, our sense of belonging.

With no one left to greet, I walked across the restaurant to my friend. Sitting across from Audrey, I glanced out the big picture window, enjoying the panorama of my town before me. Only several blocks in length and lackluster in appearance, Main Street seemed much longer and luxurious to me. Two-story buildings with stores below and, often, apartments above lined the cracked sidewalks. Their muted browns and greens felt soft, warm, and welcoming. To others, these structures might have looked faded and flat, but I overlooked their defects the way a mother might overlook the flaws in her child's face.

The waitress smiled at us. "Haven't seen you, girls, since June. What'll you have? The usual?" We both nodded.

Pop-Ins was *the* hangout, not only for South Fallsburg locals but also for the vacationers and hotel staff from the surrounding communities. During the summer, the place was jumping until the wee hours. After "show break" (when the big nightly shows ended), after the track in Monticello had run its last race, thongs of tourists, entertainers, and workers congregated at Pop-Ins. In an area known for its kosher cuisine, Pop-Ins' specialty was roast pork on garlic bread.

Just as the waitress brought over our bagels, lox and cream cheese, Ira Gold, my friend since kindergarten, came in. It struck me that Ira's cadence was the same as when we were in elementary school. He told me his grandmother had asked about me and wanted me to stop by to say hello. Of course, I told him I would love to. Our grandparents had been friends for decades.

As Audrey and I caught up over breakfast, I felt I had my town back. After talking together for over an hour, it was time to go. "See you tomorrow, same time, same place." We both smiled. Over the upcoming months, we would meet almost every morning, which made for a warm feeling.

As I walked through town, I glanced into Gold's Drug Store, one of three drugstores in town. When I was in grade school, my dad sometimes picked me up at noon and took me to Gold's for lunch. Like the other drugstores, this one has a long counter along one wall, with a Formica top with shiny edges and stools covered in red vinyl that spin around. Harry Gold, the pharmacist who also served as a counterman, smiled and waved back to me. He was kind and gentle and always remembered that I invariably ordered a BLT. I liked that.

Sitting on folding chairs on the sidewalk in front of Vince's Barber Shop, two blue-haired ladies were holding court — Gertie Gold and her best friend, my Grandma. Gertie and her husband Izzy owned the building behind them and lived upstairs. The sidewalk was Gertie's front yard, and she hosted Grandma often in the off-season. They spoke in Yiddish but switched easily to English when I stopped by to say hello. I loved the sight of them and how, when they told jokes, their blue-gray hair bobbed when they laughed.

After spending a few minutes with these two extraordinary women, I crossed the street to go to Eddy's Grocery. At the end of most days, Eddy liked to play music in the store. Early evenings when I stopped in, I often noticed a couple would stop shopping and begin to dance in the aisle. Behind the meat counter, Eddy stood with his wife, Helen. Wiping his hands on his white apron, he'd asked his customers if they'd like Dewars. Lining up several small paper cups on the counter, he poured drinks until closing. After I picked up a few things I needed, I signed the tab charging it to the hotel as I did in the Brickman coffee shop. I left the store feeling content and enveloped in my community.

By late September, crinkling leaves fell from the trees as deer crept out of the woods. In October, when hunting season commenced, the schools in the western part of Sullivan County closed. For weeks, dead deer would be seen strapped on car roofs, the hunters sporting their catch as if it were a trophy. I knew that mounds of crystalline snow would nestle in our woods in just a month or so. Winter storms would arrive, creating spectacles of light as bare branches covered with ice reached up into the frozen sky. And just as the snow began to melt in early spring, I, along with my fellow town folk, would once again eagerly await the arrival of the summer tourists.

Chapter 7

Cast of Characters, Act I

Me and Joel Rich

My world was an intricate mishmash of people. Guests and staff mingled throughout my life, coming and going, checking in, checking out. Saying goodbye was as natural as taking a breath. As a kid at the hotel day camp, I continually befriended guest children, only to have them leave after their one-week vacations. It became so ingrained early on that when I started kindergarten, I fully expected to have a whole new crew of classmates on Monday after I said goodbye to my "old" friends the previous Friday. This ephemeral nature of making acquaintances has left a lasting and positive mark on me. I am very comfortable meeting people, dealing with what's in front of me and adjusting to new situations.

Numerous "regulars" stayed at the Brickman every summer, but most of our guests came and went in a blur. They needed to be catered to, but who they were, their story and their life "in the city" stayed out of focus. The contrast between the locals' camaraderie and our guests' haze balanced out my life. As much as South Fallsburg was my centerpiece when the hotel was closed, the hotel was my foundation when we were open.

During my childhood, there was a core group of kids, relatives and friends, that I could count on being at the hotel every summer. My dad's sister, Bebe, came with her two daughters, Nina and Chichi. Our director of activities, Ben Wallach, brought his three sons, one of whom, Jeffery, was around my age and is still a dear friend. And then there was Joel, whose dad, Lenny Rich, was the manager of our reservation office and whose mom, Roz, was among my mom's closest friends.

Joel, also an only child, was the constant in my youthful summers that were full of change. Having each other to rely on made it fun and easy to get to know the cycle of other friends who came and went throughout July and August. Of course, we were too young to articulate things like "I'm glad we get to share our summers," but we instinctively knew the importance of each other in our summer lives.

This commonality, being only children, set us apart from my two cousins and Jeffery. But we all had so much fun together — simple fun, most of it taking place in the day camp: swimming, playing on the carousel, swings and monkey bars, and roasting marshmallows at the weekly campfires. My cousins and I had the privilege of lunch in the coffee shop. While the hotel kitchen was kosher, our coffee shop was not. So we got to order our favorite, BLTs with one slice of bread toasted and the other not. Then we each had an ice cream cone filled with whipped cream, and a scoop of chocolate ice cream plopped on top for dessert. Yes, my life had a lot of privileges. And hardships.

For most of Joel's childhood, he saw his father for only a few short summer months when they were all together at the hotel. Then, during the winter months, when the Brickman was closed, Lenny worked at a hotel in Lakewood, New Jersey, while Joel and Roz, his mother, returned to their home in Miami. When Roz was out with other men, her young son was alone in their apartment. At the hotel, while our mothers were together sipping Manhattans, young Joel was alone in their room waiting for the clock to strike 6 p.m. when it was time for him to walk alone to the children's dining room for dinner.

Joel's life was short. During the winter of 1972, Joel and I were just 21. Joel was living in Miami, Florida and I was living in my parent's home in South Fallsburg. My parents were in Florida for the winter.

"Patti, sit down," my father said on the phone. He sounded oddly somber. "Joel was in a car accident." I wish he hadn't been so forthright. The blue floral wallpaper in my childhood bedroom made the room feel claustrophobic.

I had not seen my childhood friend since we were 13. I had heard about him from his dad, Lenny Rich, who often complained that Joel looked like a hippy, his political views were too radical, he constantly railed about Vietnam and, if that weren't enough, he had become a vegetarian!

And now, a speeding car had rammed into his vehicle. There had been a crate of mangoes in his car's back seat, and the collision's force drove the crate into the back of his head. He was unconscious, clinging to life. Lenny immediately flew from New Jersey to his son's bedside in Miami. Roz and Lenny had not seen each other for a while, but they held onto one another for the next few days as Joel's life slipped away. He never regained consciousness. Joel was way too young to die.

That night that I learned of his death, it was below zero outside, but the walls of our home were closing in on me. I walked into town, my hands tucked into my parka, memories of Joel rushing in. "You're younger than I am," he loved to tease, being all of two weeks older. For the 50-plus years that have passed, I have lit a candle every May 13, his birthday. This was my first harrowing glimpse at the fragility of life.

When Joel and I were kids, my mom and Roz, Joel's mom, spent many a late afternoon together. "Tell her not every day, Rae," my dad would scold. "I can't stand her, always drunk and useless around the hotel." But at 5:00 p.m., just minutes after my dad went back to work, I could hear the unsteady click of Roz's heels on our steps.

"No need to knock, Roz. Come on in." My mother already had their Manhattans prepared. Roz settled herself into the cozy round chair that spun in all directions. "Fill her up," Roz said, eagerly awaiting their first round of drinks. My mother sat on the red couch facing her. They both tossed off their shoes in unison.

Roz had banana-blond hair, coiffed closely to her face, allowing her curls to hug her head handsomely. She often wore a tight-fitting black number that accentuated her ample bust, an asset she seemed to enjoy displaying, often around my Uncle Murray. She would invariably fish for a compliment on her latest attempt at fashion, frequently noting that "They are wearing this these days." It became a standard joke for my mother to reply, "And who are 'they'?"

My mom always had stylish clothes, often in bright colors and silky fabrics, so inconsistent with her depression and anxiety. She adored her herringbone blazer that she wore with stylish trousers and her slinky green sequin dress. Eyes turned when she entered a room.

Few noticed Roz when she was sober, but when the alcohol had reached the tipping point, she would reveal her drunkenness as if uncovering a boudoir portrait. On special occasions and holidays, she would add pills to the mix. Those nights she could be found in the office where her husband Lenny worked, plopped next to him, just waiting for the right moment to pick a fight. With the words slurring from her lips, she'd begin, "You son of a bitch." Lenny had long since learned to ignore her, and his silence would bring her to tears. Then, struggling to sit upright, she'd go into a blistering attack about the most intimate details of their lives. Eventually, someone would escort her back to her room, but never Lenny. Often it was Uncle Murray.

I imagine my mom was grateful for her friendship, a pact forged on maudlin sentiment and frightened laughter. Several pictures remain from those years, many of Roz by herself, some with my mom, and a few of them with their friends, couples that would frequent the hotel, in various groupings. You can see them lined up outside the nightclub, posing stiffly next to each other, mates alongside spouses and smiling for the camera. And there to the far left was Roz, all dressed up and standing alone.

As reservation manager, Lenny Rich was one of the most critical Brickman employees. He began working at the hotel as a young man. He was meek, seemingly living in a haze, taking abuse from his boss, Murray, and his wife. But Lenny could be charming. He often had a cigar in hand while imitating Maurice Chevalier singing *Thank Heaven for Little Girls*, and he was good. Lenny could sound like he spoke French fluently, but if you listened carefully, you realized he was speaking fluent double-talk. He was gentle and sad, carrying himself as if he had misplaced his spine. Working alongside Lenny was pleasant, as long as Murray or Roz weren't around. As the "girls" in the office took reservations, they would hand over the completed reservation forms to Lenny. Then he would assign the rooms and keep records of how many rooms were available at any given time. He could be counted on to send a family to a room that was occupied, and then cover his mistakes with a convoluted excuse.

Lenny was responsible for placing 600 guests into 300 bedrooms. Of course, back then, keeping track of reservations was done without computers. At the front desk, Lenny's room chart was hidden from view, which was deliberate because his system was archaic. He had little slips of paper that represented individual rooms grouped by the buildings on the property. Each slip bore the guest's name, check-in and check-out days, and requested room categories. On a busy check-in day, Lenny often juggled several slips of paper, forgetting to write down the room he would assign to them. Sometimes he overbooked. Sometimes he thought all rooms were booked, only to find out several were open.

More than once I would open the side door to the office only to stand quietly in the doorway while Murray was in the middle of one of his tirades directed at Lenny. I'd trade knowing glances with Betty, our convention manager, and Frances, a reservation clerk, as Murray screamed something along the lines of, "For days, we've been turning away people, and now you tell me we have rooms open. You son of a bitch, how can you do this to me? You're eating my kishkes out!" When Murray mentioned his kishkes, you knew it was bad. Lenny would remain silent. I wondered if he secretly wanted to confront Murray in his convoluted French double talk.

There was one other person in the office. Sandy — Murray's mistress and then some. Depending on her mood, she would subtly egg Murray on with a supportive glance or distract him with some concern. On the verge of a coughing spell, Murray would look over to Sandy. With a certain intimacy, she'd say, "Mur, come here; I have something to discuss with you." He obeyed. As if on cue, the two women taking reservations resumed their work. Lenny adjusted his tie and returned to assigning rooms for Sunday's check-in.

Chapter 8

My Uncle, His Wife and His Mistress

Uncle Murray. How many times did one of our flustered employees exclaim, "Your Uncle Murray!" as if I were responsible for him? A hands-on employer, he left his fingerprints on all aspects of the work he doled out. He trusted his judgment exclusively and micromanaged even the most menial tasks, orchestrating the staff to create an audience for himself. He deliberately hired people who needed a little prestige, a place to call home. It could be a comedic genius stunted by stage fright or an entertainer thirsty for a stage. These were people he could lord over. Indeed, Murray was the counterpart to my dad, who was a man of integrity, poise, humor, whimsy and wisdom. As one of my friends once joked, "It's like Ben and Murray were born Siamese twins, and when they were separated, Ben got the heart."

While Murray was charismatic, his wardrobe was decidedly not. Often spending part of the winter months deep-sea fishing in Cozumel,

Mexico, he was influenced by the local style of dress: white cotton shirts with embossed stripes down the front, Larry King-style suspenders, and a brown sweater jacket fit for an academic or intellectual, but he was neither. He was bright and could display an extraordinary sense of humor, but his dress spoke to his blunt practicality. He had a large stomach and a flat rear, and the suspenders simply held up his pants.

Murray's true passion in life had been to be an entertainer. He studied law at St. John's University in New York City, but upon graduating, he wanted to be a stand-up comedian in the Catskills. He probably would have excelled, but his father needed him at the hotel. In addition, the Brickman family was just starting to fracture, and Murray's new law degree was essential in restructuring the hotel and the family. Uncle Murray ultimately became the hotel's surround sound and played a unique, if not always pleasant, role during my Hotel Brickman years.

Murray and his wife, Helen, spent their winters at their home in Miami. I loved their house, with its cool shades of gray, the backyard pool and the dock. I used to play with their neighbors' kids, swimming all afternoon until our parents pried us out of the water as the sun melted over Key Biscayne. The only thing better than the pool was going out with Murray on his boat. He'd pack a Kentucky Fried Chicken lunch, and we'd plow along the Intracoastal Waterway, finding the right spot to anchor and munch on the crispy feast while Murray fished.

When I was young, I loved visiting them during the winter holidays. But I wasn't able to visit them during the winter of 1960. I broke my leg skating at the Pines Hotel, one of our friendly competitors. For the next three months, I was cooped up in bed, my leg itching in a cast from my upper thigh to my toes. Every day but Sunday during my convalescence, I received a letter or card, postmarked Miami, signed by Uncle Murray. Some of the letters had funny pictures drawn of places we had visited in Florida. When I opened the cards in which my uncle had written upside down or backward, I forgot about being restricted to my bed. It took me hours to decipher his notes with a mirror in hand.

My Uncle Murray. The family custom was to refer to our aunt and uncle as dear, sweet, kind Uncle Murray and mean old Aunt Helen. He wasn't always sweet; she was never mean. He was wonderful to me when I was a child but resentful of me when I grew up. But he was my dad's brother, and they had a bond and a love for one another that even Sandy, Murray's trouble-making mistress, could not break.

One afternoon, when I was 12 or 13, I walked into my parents' bedroom. It was all dark. I turned on the light, and the red décor of the room surprised me as if I were seeing it for the first time. I felt dizzy as I looked over at my mother, lying motionless across their bed. She did not look up at me. "Get my dad!" I screamed into the phone at the switchboard operator. Within minutes my dad and uncle ran into the bedroom to find me shaking and my mother immobile.

I raced to my room, which was adjacent to my parents. I left the door open a crack, hoping to hear what was being said. Suddenly my mother was wailing. It would have been soulful if she had been singing, but the sounds coming from her now were eerie and frightening. I sighed a bit of relief when she finally sat up. The brothers cleaned the cuts on her hands and wrapped them gently in bandages. "I'll take her for a ride. I'll talk to her," Murray said. "Have someone drive a car around." My father wordlessly went along with this plan. They wrapped her in a sweater and escorted her to the car. My mother clung to both of them.

I lay wide awake in my bed for hours, punctuated by short visits from my dad. I saw the strain in his eyes telling me this was serious indeed. When Murray finally brought her home, it was very late. So I feigned sleep when my dad came to check in on me. It wouldn't be until many years later that I began to understand my mother's depression and anxiety and how Paula's death and the lie about her age likely contributed to my mother's mental state.

When I was in my late twenties, my dad shared with me what he had learned about that night. My mom had been walking over the bridge at the hotel heading toward our apartment. Blood was dripping from her hand, tears coursing down her cheeks. The bridge, traversing the road that divided the Brickman property, led to the nightclub. It was lined with photos of the entertainers who had appeared at the hotel. My mother had ripped one photo off the wall — of a beautiful young female singer — with such fury that she had broken the glass in the frame and cut her hands. I never found out why. Perhaps she was jealous. Rumors were that the singer was one of the many women with whom my uncle had been "extra fond."

Murray's raspy cough would precede him as he opened the glass doors to the lobby each morning. He'd walk over to the front desk and cough into the face of the young switchboard operator before asking, "Any messages for me, dear?" He was already turning around and on his way to the dining room when she said, "No." If I happened to be in the lobby during this ritual, he would nod in my direction, barely acknowledging me. I never got used to his attitude toward me as an adult.

"Everything going okay, Karl?" he'd asked the maître d'. Karl Tagman had a distinct accent left over from his childhood in Hungary. He had spent his teenage years outrunning the Nazis during World War II. It was well known to most of the staff that Karl had nightmares that made him scream as if he were still fleeing certain death. As a result, he would often cringe when a guest was dressed in a horizontally striped dress, bringing him back to the horrific years of the Holocaust.

After greeting Karl, Murray would slide into his seat at the family table while motioning to his waiter, Tony, for his first cup of coffee, brought without delay. "Your usual, boss?" Tony would ask, although he already knew Murray invariably would have two eggs over easy and a fresh bagel with a schmear of cream cheese and just a small piece of lox.

Sandy routinely walked in a few minutes after he was seated, having been waiting for him in the dining room lobby. She was stalking him, in a sense. Sandy wasn't welcome to sit at the family table unless he invited her to sit down. He would hardly look up as she strolled in, a cigarette dangling from his lips while another sat burning in the ashtray. Noticing the two, he'd smile. He was a five-pack-a-day man, and his cough came from deep within, like one of his diatribes.

Sandy Merle was of medium height with dark hair atop a round face. She smoked as much as Mur, as she liked to call him. She would pick up his second cigarette in the ashtray as she reached for her coffee. Sandy worked for the agency that booked all the acts for our nightly entertainment. She had a bedroom at the hotel, a WOB, without bath, (her bathroom was down the hall) and a small office just off the main reservation office.

She had found her way into Murray's world when she was about 25, and he was in his mid-50s. This was not a father/daughter friendship. Sandy was not Murray's first mistress, but she was his longest and his last. My Aunt Helen seemed resigned to the many other women with whom she had to share her husband.

Sandy was resented by almost everyone who came into her orbit, but that wasn't because she was Murray's mistress. It was because she was, simply put, mean-spirited. Sandy had successfully established herself as Murray's sidekick (with benefits) as she entrenched herself deeper into the fabric of the hotel. Sandy isolated and influenced Murray. He seemed unaware she was doing this.

Technically, Sandy was supposed to book the acts for the hotel, but her sphere of influence increased as she accumulated years at the resort. Gradually, Murray's ongoing relationship with her alienated many vital members of our staff — and, most importantly, my dad. The two brothers had been close all their lives, able to discuss anything, but now my dad knew that whatever he said to Murray would almost immediately be shared with Sandy.

Extramarital affairs and sexual harassment were, unfortunately, almost acceptable back when Murray was on the prowl. His reputation with women preceded his marriage, but being married did not curtail his behavior. I knew some of his women, even liked some of them — but not Sandy. She created a wedge between the two brothers and made things uncomfortable and unpleasant for many of the key staff, including me. I resented him for that and how it impacted my dad and our family and business.

When Sandy became such an irritant, we had a group that we called the United Front Against Tanta (*tanta* is Yiddish for "aunt"). It was comprised of several very close friends who worked at the hotel for many years. Most of them had started when I was a teenager (they were at least 10 years older than me), but by the time I was in my twenties, we all were very close. The group included Larry Strickler, our director of activities; Shelly, his wife; Mel Simon, the master of ceremonies; and Rochelle Kovar, the captain in the dining room.

We had a code word, "bulletin," and without the luxury of texting, we managed to gather quickly once the word was out. A bulletin could be in response to finding out that Sandy was trying to oust an employee, usually another woman, or if tense words had been overheard between Murray and Sandy. The final bulletin came in 2006, years after the hotel was sold, when we found out that Sandy had passed away in her late 60s. Soon after hearing the news, my dad met with a business associate who asked why my dad looked so peaceful and happy. Without missing a beat, my dad explained, "Sandy died."

I can't say I was sorry to hear of her passing; during her reign, she poisoned the atmosphere behind the scenes at the hotel. I witnessed her create a wedge between the "boys." I watched Murray pull away from his brother and business partner, sidestepping his ideas and opinions, relying more on her than him. Our family was being torn apart. Many of the staff had to bear the difficult years when Sandy manipulated things in ways antithetical to the dignity that my family had created for their employees.

And Helen had to endure. Murray met Helen Levy in 1938 when, just out of secretarial school, she landed a job with the hotel's booking agent, George Kutton. The pungent smell of George's cigars made the young Helen think about finding another job — until Murray began to pour on the charm. But she would prove to be a most delicate conquest.

What started with a finely tuned sense of smell would eventually medically escalate. Her menstrual cycle left her weak and in pain as a young woman, causing her to spend several days a month in bed. As an older woman, severe rheumatoid arthritis confined her to her bed for weeks. She held court from their bedroom, ordering food from the hotel kitchen or her maid, buying clothes from her favorite local store and stocks from her Merrill Lynch broker.

Helen had the hotel construction crew build a small but luxurious wading pool adjoining her bedroom. She claimed that she needed it to ease the pain from her arthritis, but as far as I know, she rarely used it. But my daughter Jo Anna preferred her Aunt Helen's pool to the hotel's outdoor, indoor and kiddy pools. Some of the staff, who had never actually seen Helen since she, like my mother, spent most of her time in the confines of her bedroom, joked that Helen was long dead and that this new extension was really a mausoleum.

"I'm pre-cancerous," Helen blithely told me one day as I sat on the chair in the corner of her bedroom. "I'm taking gold shots," she bragged as if she were talking about jewelry. Her maid, Adela, was a short Guatemalan woman with gray streaks in her hair who spoke a mixture of English and Spanish. She had worked for Helen for so long that she had begun to take on her employer's mannerisms and ailments. From her bed, Helen had taught Adela all of the recipes she had learned growing up in the warmth of her mother's kitchen. Adela could whip up hot beef borscht or braised breast of veal surrounded by prunes and apricots as if she, too, had family who immigrated here from Eastern Europe.

Murray and Helen were married in 1939, two years after my parents. Helen, who saw herself as a businesswoman, felt she needed to sculpt a place for herself at the hotel. According to my mother, the sisters-in-law had several run-ins right at the start. One memorable day Helen marched into the office, saw my mother typing away and felt this beyond her station as a primarily stay-at-home wife. So Helen picked up the typewriter and tossed it into the garbage. My mother called it "the worst thing that could ever happen to me. Murray had to find someone from Brooklyn, no less!" I do not know Helen's side of the story, but I can imagine it was very different from my mother's version.

With their spouses feuding, the brothers had to find a way to reinvent their personal and working relationships. Although their wives barely spoke to each other after the typewriter incident, my father and uncle were able to maintain a trusting personal and business relationship. Until Sandy came onto the scene.

In 1973, when I was about 23, I started to work as a reservation clerk in the office, which meant that Murray was my boss. He had been wonderful to me when I was a child, but he had grown distinctly distant at this point. My uncle struggled with me because I refused to be one of his obedient minions. When I felt it necessary, I questioned him and his authority. We had a major confrontation at least once a year. At times like that, I had to be quick on my feet and decisive with my words.

We always had our annual arguments in his office, with me standing over him as he sat at his desk. One day I heard myself blurting out to him, "You resent me because my dad had a child, and you never did!" He looked up at me, startled by my honesty. He didn't say a word, and I took this as having unearthed a painful truth. Then, as I had done on other occasions, I turned around and walked out of the office, closing the door behind me. These encounters taught me to carefully choose my words and how to exit on a strong note.

Chapter 9

Cast of Characters, Act II

Chubby Lenz, Lenny Rich, Murray Posner

While guests and most staff came and went, there were several men, women and their families who spent a lifetime of summers working for us, while others had long runs of five, ten years or more, offering me a sense of stability and continuity.

For almost 30 years, Betty Spear worked at the hotel. She excelled when she was our bookkeeper. After ten years in the role, Murray wanted her in his entourage of female employees, so he promoted her to convention manager.

Betty had the qualities Murray looked for in an employee. She was loyal, hesitant to make any decisions independently, and flattered when her boss flirted with her. Betty made an attractive appearance: Her clothes were always color coordinated, her shoes and bag matched. Her short blond hair was teased to perfection, and her manicured hands were slightly stained from nicotine. She was a single woman who had a long relationship with a married man we nicknamed Nervous Nat. He would frequently call to check up on her, and I suspect he did not trust her to be faithful to him, a married man.

Often you could hear Murray impatiently cajoling her. "Betty, for a few hours after lunch, make some phone calls!" She'd nod and promise. She was good at nodding and promising, but she had no interest in selling. She never quite got the hang of being a convention manager, but she stayed in this position until we sold the hotel.

And then there was Chubby, my all-time favorite person. My dad met Chubby in 1928 when they both were picking up guests at the railroad station in South Fallsburg. Chubby was working at the Plaza Hotel. My dad saw something special in Chubby and asked him to come to work at the hotel.

Like Uncle Murray, Chubby aspired to be a comedian but never became one. Born Abraham Lenz in 1912, he earned the name Chubby as the pounds collected around his waist. Chubby slipped into various roles around the hotel on an as-needed basis without having an official title and not needing one. He might show up as the captain in the nightclub or in the main office taking reservations. At the front desk, when irate guests came to complain, Chubby could always calm them down.

"Mrs. Schwartz, what's the problem?" Chubby would say as he stepped up to the counter at the front desk. Leaning in as he began to address the guest, he looked the extremely annoyed woman right in the eye. Then he'd tenderly touch her hand just as she placed a soiled blouse on the countertop. "Tell me, dear," he'd say, "just what has made you so upset." With her anger evaporating, she'd begin, "Well, my waiter, this morning, he spilled orange juice all over my pink blouse." Chubby would remove his hand from hers, knowing he had ingratiated himself to her. She then pulled the soiled top out of her bag and placed it in front of Chubby. "Oh, how terrible," he commiserated, "Let me give you $10 to have the blouse cleaned. Or better yet, give me the blouse, and I will take care of it for you." He worked his reassuring allure against the full spectrum of annoyances that our guests complained about.

He had a sweet character and an over-the-top sense of humor. He once convinced a guest that she could return to the Bronx by hopping on a submarine that, on Sundays right after breakfast, picked up passengers at the deep end of the outdoor pool. And sure enough, she showed up right on time, suitcase in hand.

But when it came to being a comic, Chubby could not walk on stage without downing a drink and then another until his fear subsided along with his routine. Sober, he could convince you of just about anything, but drunk, he could barely remember his name. He used his comedic talents to write material for other comedians, some very well-known, like Buddy Hackett.

Even Murray couldn't resist Chubby's charms, giving him a place to call home, a career and a "family" who loved him. My uncle was easier on Chubby than he was on the others who sought to be in the inner circle. And in return, Chubby was exceedingly loyal to his friend and employer.

When Chubby was in his late 50s, he fell in love with a young Chinese-American pharmacist. Murray and Helen decided that Eve was not an appropriate partner for him and would not allow their long-time friend to bring her onto the hotel grounds. They made Chubby rent a room nearby. He had to order extra food from the staff dining room that he carefully wrapped up and brought to her. Murray would ride Chubby mercilessly about how mismatched he felt they were. Chubby took this abuse with little outward resistance, but it sickened and saddened me and my dad. While still in love with Eve, at the end of October 1975, Chubby died suddenly of a heart attack. He was 63.

Chapter 10

Two New Bellhops

Superintendent of services Rocky Black

April Fool's Day, 1965. It was a chilly day, no longer winter but not yet spring. As I got off the school bus, I noticed the grass beginning to peek through the melting snow. The lilacs would soon bud. I walked down the long driveway of the hotel toward the Main Building. We were having the first check-in of the season.

Opening the glass doors to the lobby, I waved hello to Rocky, the superintendent of service. Rocky had worked for us all my life. He was family to me, another one of the staff who was a constant in my life.

Rocky looked like he stepped out of a black-and-white 1940s film noir, especially when on duty at the lobby service desk, with his compact, chiseled features, dapper suit and a husky cough courtesy of the constant cigarette in hand. He was in charge of the bellhops, a crew of eight young men, and I was eager to meet the two recruits he had most recently hired. As I walked past Rocky, I saw them, one dark-haired, the other red-haired, dressed in bellhop uniforms, kelly green trousers and jackets with candy-cane stripes up the front. "I thought they'd make me wear a matching green beret," I overheard the dark-haired one say. The red-headed one nodded in agreement as he puffed on his Camel.

I was intrigued with Michael Rothman, the dark-haired bellhop, from the moment I saw him. He seemed charming and intelligent, his smile effectively concealing the twisted agony I would eventually come to know all too well. At first, neither of us noticed the symmetry of our slender faces, the blue of our eyes and our brown hair. But, before long, we grew accustomed to hearing, "You look so much alike."

Bob Speer drew my attention with his crisp red hair and freckled face. He seemed more stable than Michael, and I was drawn to that. He was a student at Queens College, studying to become an accountant. I found his nervous foot tapping a kind of dance, and his sassy humor was adorable.

1965 was my second season as a "real" teenager, and the hotel had become a buffet of potential boyfriends. I was a risk, of course, being the boss's daughter, but I also was cute with a burgeoning sense of self, and the young men paid enough attention for me to hone my flirting skills. The summer before, when I was 14, my first crush came fast and furious, and my parents watched over me as if my virginity was hanging by a thread.

Joey Bellomo worked at the hotel for many years and was the cutest soda jerk I had ever seen. He was also very talented and sang in the staff talent shows on Thursday nights. I never missed a show. As the casino darkened, Joey was still in the coffee shop. Finally, the music to "My Boy Bill" from *Carousel* began. A spotlight pointed to the rear entrance. The door opened, and Joey swaggered in, his white apron hugging his muscular, slender body. As he stepped into the nightclub, the audience turned, his strong voice mesmerizing the room.

When I heard Joey's younger brother Dominic was coming up to work in the coffee shop, I had a crush on him before we met. Toward the end of the summer of 1964, my dad caught us making out in the ping-pong room. To my complete humiliation, my father refused to rehire him for the 1965 season. The word began to get out that being my boyfriend meant just one season at the Brickman, something I was teased about relentlessly. I was determined to show those needlers that I was not the spoiled, overly protected kid they perceived me to be.

By the summer of '65, I was working in the office as a switchboard operator and front-desk clerk, with a firm curfew of 11 p.m.. By not rehiring Dominic, my parents thought that perhaps they need not worry too much about their little girl falling in love. They were wrong.

After that first meeting with the new bellhops, I went into the office and checked my schedule for the weekend. I would work primarily at the front desk, so I knew I'd get to see them often. About half an hour later, I announced I was going to the service desk to see my dog, Peppy. My real reason: to continue appraising the new recruits.

Peppy had a serious crush on Rocky and loved to hang out at the service desk. Her tail began wagging as I approached her. I pulled down the hem of my miniskirt as I knelt awkwardly to rub her belly. Bobby, the redhead, smiled at me. Feeling the eyes of the two bellhops on me as I petted my dog, I realized I needed a game plan to stand back up. I held on to my skirt as if it were a religious symbol and somehow got back onto my feet.

"This is Patti Posner, the boss's daughter," Rocky announced as I straightened my skirt. I felt a familiar awkward blush at this introduction. Why couldn't he just say, "This is Patti," and let them think I was one of them? But "boss's daughter" inevitably trailed my name until we sold the hotel.

I was hanging around the service desk when Joanie rang the call bell at the front desk, indicating she needed a bellhop to take a couple to their room. "You're up," Rocky said to Bobby, who flew off his seat. At the front desk, he stood as instructed, his feet hip-width apart, hands on his side while waiting to find out what room he'd have to schlep the guest's luggage to. The next day was the big check-in for Passover, so this was an excellent opportunity for the new guys to learn the ropes.

By Memorial Day, the weekend of my 15th birthday, Michael was my friend, and Bobby was my boyfriend. By July 4th, they were both up for the summer. Both lived in New York City, Bobby in Queens and Michael in the Bronx. The names of the boroughs, which I had learned from registering our guests, were practically all I knew about the city. But I was learning other things.

As I honed my flirting skills with bellhops and waiters, I also learned about work ethics. I became a crackerjack switchboard operator (think Lily Tomlin as Ernestine from the 1960s show (*Laugh-In*) and front-desk clerk, giving change, answering a myriad of questions from our guests and handling all sorts of problems, from a dollop of sour cream on a sweater to more substantial matters, such as a mistake on a bill or a missed phone call. Or someone was falling ill or suddenly dropping dead.

Morris Kaplan died in his seat in the Main Dining Room. He simply slumped over, his head landing on a bagel. Getting Morris out of the room without causing a commotion was not easy. My dad and Uncle Murray were at the family table. The dining room captain calmly whispered the news to them. The two brothers casually walked over to the dearly departed, nodded at each other, hoisted Morris up, and with an arm dangling around each brother's neck, they "walked" him out of the dining room.

Once I mastered the art of the switchboard, I then became adept as a front-desk clerk. I quickly learned how to register guests, entering their names and addresses in my neat cursive handwriting, as my dad had taught me as a child in anticipation of my eventually taking on this job. Check-in day required a lot of patience, a couple of pens and legible handwriting. I didn't know New York City at all, but I knew Bay Parkway meant Brooklyn, N.Y. 11204.

The other requirement with registering guests was to guess the age of those we were registering. As a teenager, they all looked old to me. Some were old, 45, and some ancient, 73 (my current age). When there were enough registration cards, I sent them to the dining room, where the maitre d' sorted them out by age and assigned guests to their tables with eight or ten other guests. Rarely did a couple sit alone at a table. Catskill guests who started as strangers often became lifetime friends.

I knew very little about our guests or their city life. I only knew that their week at our hotel was a highlight of their year. Their vacations would fill their lives with memories for a lifetime. Now decades later, former guests and staff have told me countless times about their fond and fun memories of their time at the Hotel Brickman. This is an honor and a blessing, and it fills me with awe and joy to know that a place I got to call home has such meaning to so many.

Chapter 11

Marriage # 1

June 1, 1969

On June 1, 1969, when I was only 19, I married my first bellhop, Robert Norman Speer. My mother had one goal for me — not college, as I wish it had been, but marriage. I did go to C.W. Post for almost two semesters, but once Bobby proposed in December 1968 and with a diamond ring on my finger, I decided college was not for me. I have more marriages under my belt, three, than children or college degrees. I have one each.

With marriage came a job promotion: I was now taking reservations. From an early age, Grandma and my father prepared me for what they perceived as my role at the hotel, office work. On my first day taking reservations, I knew the answers to any question a prospective guest might ask. I could tell a parent about their child's experience in day camp or the teen group, assuring them that their precious son or daughter would be well taken care of, just as I had been. Having grown up at the hotel, I was ready to take reservations.

My parents threw us a large wedding. Bobby and I were married on the stage of the hotel's nightclub and the reception was held in the dining room. We were married on the Sunday of Memorial Day weekend. A very busy weekend. Check-out time was 3 p.m., but on this Sunday, we asked our guests to check out at 1 p.m. We were married early that evening. Murray helped set up the nightclub and dining room, but he did not come to my wedding because of the animosity between his wife and my mother.

Toward the end of the reception, I was having drinks with a few friends in the Lobby Bar just off the dining room. Suddenly Michael rushed in. "I'm sorry, but I can't stay," he told me. "I just got a phone call from my dad. He was beaten up by a loan shark and is in the hospital. I have to go." I had no idea what to say. First, I didn't even know what a loan shark was. I was still a virgin on many levels.

"Bye, Mrs. Speer," he smiled and winked at me as he ran off.

Michael would have to borrow money to pay off his father's debt. Gambling and drugs were a part of Michael's life. Many of his friends were doing drugs and had been for years. By the time I met him, a few had already died from popping, snorting or shooting. For me, such things took place only in movies. My friends had barely relinquished their Barbie dolls to immerse themselves in rock 'n' roll. They weren't rolling joints, not yet, anyway.

One afternoon in the first few weeks of my marriage, I was sitting on the curb in front of the Main Building with Michael. "I made a mistake," I confessed. I got up and walked away before he could respond. I'm not sure he even heard me, as he most likely was stoned.

During the second year of our marriage, Bob was in the Army Reserves and was called away for a month of training. I was on my own that month for the first time, living alone in our apartment in Monticello. Once I experienced being on my own, I realized I did not need to be a "Mrs.". My marriage to Bobby proved short-lived, and on June 9, 1972 (after just three years and eight days), we were divorced.

That summer, Michael's friend, Kathy Peterson, came to work at the hotel. They were both in college together in Wisconsin. I first heard of Kathy in 1971, when she was taking a semester in Sierra

Leone, Africa. She was a true free spirit, a Midwesterner, independent in ways I could not even imagine. My only time away from home had been to Los Angeles on our honeymoon.

Kathy became my closest friend that year, and we remained close for many decades. By summer's end, she had convinced me to join her on a road trip to her college town of Oshkosh, Wisconsin, to pick up her boyfriend, Brian Moushey. From there, we'd go to her hometown of St. Croix Falls and to Colorado after that.

Later that fall, Kathy and Brian planned to spend a few months in Europe, and Kathy wanted me to join them there. This trip was crazy, my going out west and then to Europe with a person I just met and a total stranger. But it was 1972. Adventure was in the air.

On a cool September morning, Kathy and I filled my car full of our essentials and headed west. First to Oshkosh, where I faced my initial taste of anti-Semitism. The city was known for beer drinking, and our first stop was a bar where Kathy was a regular. While standing at the bar, a student who knew I was Kathy's New York friend approached and asked, "You're Jewish? What does your father own?" Growing up in the Catskills shielded me from anti-Semitic comments like this. However, I was beginning to find my voice, something I had only practiced with Uncle Murray. So, I looked at him, right in his big blue eyes, and replied, "A resort hotel." Then I turned around and walked away.

Kathy, Brian and I next headed to St. Croix Falls, a small town in Northern Wisconsin that reminded me so much of South Fallsburg. As I had been in Oshkosh, I was the only Jewish person in town, but Kathy's family and friends were very welcoming. Even though we were different in many ways, I began to see that Kathy and I shared the experience of small-town living, embraced and encircled by friends and family. After a few days with her family, we continued west to Colorado. I was beginning to experience independence and my adult voice. With each mile that passed, the world opened up a bit more for me.

After a week of fun times in Colorado, we headed back east. The trip to Europe came next; Kathy and Brian left a few weeks before me, so this would be my first trip alone and my second plane ride.

My parents took me to the airport. I cannot imagine how my dad thought it was OK for me to travel across the ocean to travel with a college friend of Michael and her boyfriend, whom I hardly knew. On top of that, I would not find out where Kathy and Brian were staying in Rome until I arrived. After landing in Rome, I would have to find my way to the American Embassy to retrieve a note from my friends telling me what pension they were staying in. Not even in a hotel, but a hostel or pension. And yet. My dad took me to the airport. He trusted me more than I trusted myself. He confessed to me years later that he had applied for his first passport before my trip, just in case I needed him.

Fear overcame me as we entered JFK. Once at the international gate, I darted off to a corner of the terminal and sat on the floor in a fetal position, clutching my purse. My parents followed. Tears were streaming down my cheeks. My father sat beside me as my mother hovered over us. I expected my dad to wrap his arms around me and take me home. "You'll get on the plane," my dad said with serene assurance. My mother was silent, perhaps relating to my distress. Then, he suggested he'd have my recent ex-husband, Bob, meet me in Rome the next day. At the time, it sounded like a plan.

Meekly, I boarded the plane and immediately scanned my fellow passengers in case any of them turned out to be terrorist hijackers. There had already been 11 such hijackings in 1972, so it wasn't out of the question. (It wasn't easy being brought up by a mother who was agoraphobic.) The flight proved uneventful, and as I deplaned safely in Rome, there was an announcement that the buses going from the airport to the city were on strike. recommending that four people share a cab for the trip into the city. I had never even been to New York City on my own, and here I was, alone in Rome, with vague plans on how to meet my friends. So now I had to find three strangers to share a cab with. But then I remembered that strangers coming and going were a part of my Brickman life. I could do this.

A new me emerged as I stepped into the crisp fall Italian day. And there I was, escorting three other people into a cab. As we settled in for the ride, I comfortably slipped into my hotel-host mode, making chit-chat with my cab mates. Then, as improbable as it sounds, the young man sitting next to me noted my name was Posner and asked if I was familiar with the Brickman Hotel. He had once been a waiter there.

I said goodbye to my fellow passengers, feeling proud of myself. And then, there I was, standing in front of the American Embassy. It felt like I was walking into a grand hotel as I approached what I took as their front desk. "I am here to collect a note from my friend, Kathy Peterson," I told a woman behind the desk.

She looked at me the way I might look at a guest who expected to board a submarine at the deep end of our swimming pool. "I am sorry," she said, "people do not leave notes for friends at the embassy." I walked outside, not knowing what to do next. If I had had a cell phone, I would have asked my dad to buy me a ticket on the next flight home.

Since that was not an option, I walked outside into the sunshine and stood there, unsure of what to do. Before long, the worried look on my face prompted a young man with long stringy hair and a sweet smile to come over to me. "You look lost," he said. I explained my situation, and he said, "Not the American Embassy, the American Express office!" He generously escorted me to the American Express office, where I retrieved the note from Kathy with the address of their pension. He helped me find the pension. I asked him to join us at dinner that night, but he begged off, and I never saw him again.

Already a few weeks into their trip, Kathy and Brian were so welcoming to me but were not enchanted with the idea of Bob joining us for two weeks. They decided to go to Florence for the first week and then meet Bob and me on the island of Crete. Bob arrived the next day, and when he left two weeks later, I was glad to see him go. The security I thought I needed was not there in him; it was inside me.

After visiting the island of Crete, Kathy, Brian and I spent six weeks traveling through Italy, Greece, Paris and Amsterdam. Our trip offered me a sense of freedom, adventure and independence. It was the time of my life.

Years later, my dad often sent me letters or emails, even though we lived so close to each other and spoke on the phone daily. The one I treasure the most, written years after my European trip, says, *"When you went to Europe for the first time, it was like a part of you was leaving forever. When you came back, you were all grown up. Your cross-country trip to Colorado was also a traumatic experience for me, knowing you were out there with strange boys, not knowing where you were. I then knew you could survive without me. It made me grow up too. It's not easy being a parent."*

But it wasn't so easy being a daughter, either. I returned in the dark days of December, divorced, living alone in my parents' home (they were in Florida) and without a job until the hotel reopened in the spring. I was in my childhood bedroom, not knowing what to do with myself. Most of my friends were in college, as was Michael. We spoke every few weeks. A new soft tone to his voice let me know he was falling in love with me. I had already realized that I loved him. While he was home for a weekend, we decided to meet in the city. I drove down with excitement and trepidation, knowing that our seven-year friendship was about to change.

I saw him before he noticed me. He was hunched over, trying to shield himself from the wind signaling a winter day. Smiling when he saw me, he motioned that there was a parking spot up the block. We did not kiss hello, yet we looked at each other with a sense of knowing what was to come.

Walking into the lobby of his building on Wallace Avenue, we stepped into the empty elevator. I felt his hand touch mine as the door closed. He moved toward me. We stood silently as the elevator took us to the fifth floor. As we stepped into the hallway, he took my hand, and we walked to his parent's apartment.

I remember feeling his firm flesh as he pressed me gently against the front door. Feeling the doorknob in my back, I adjusted myself because all I wanted to feel was Michael. The thick drapes in the living room did not allow much light to filter into the vestibule where we embraced. "Come with me to the bedroom," he whispered. I followed him into the small bedroom he shared with his siblings when he was home.

"My mom's at work and my dad must be at the track." I was no longer thinking about such practical things. The warmth of his blue comforter greeted me as I sat next to him on his bed. As we made love that brisk afternoon, the sun shone through the curtains, casting a shadow across us as we lay in his bed. That night I drove back home, and I waited out the winter until the hotel reopened and my parents returned. My life was about to change.

Chapter 12

My Second Marriage to a Bellhop

A year later, on March 18, 1974, I walked down Wallace Avenue in the Bronx, eager to see Michael's smiling face. We were to be married in just ten days, and once again, I would be fulfilling my mother's dream for me to be someone's wife. I expected him to be downstairs to meet me, that we would share a kiss in the elevator and spend the afternoon making plans for our life together.

I felt alien in this corner of the Bronx, Pelham Parkway, where Michael and his younger siblings, Arthur and Marsha, had grown up. Their mother, Bertha, slept in the primary bedroom, and most nights their dad, Moshe, slept on the convertible couch in the living room. Each morning the couple would leave together, Bertha to her job as a secretary at a small company nearby, Moshe to his place in line at the local OTB parlor.

Although I was mildly annoyed that Michael wasn't there to escort me to his apartment, I fell gratefully into his arms when he opened the door. He greeted me warmly but made no excuse for not coming downstairs; instead, he took my hand and walked me into the kitchen. He picked up some items and headed toward the bathroom. I followed.

I watched as he tied a pale-yellow rubber strap around his left tricep. With his right hand, he tapped the vein in the crux of his elbow. Then he lit a match and placed it under a filthy spoon containing his toxic liquid. With the skill of a surgeon, he drew the liquid into the syringe and carefully put the needle into his bulging vein. All at once, his blue eyes dulled, his dark pupils shrank to pinpoints, and his eyelids drooped. The needle fell from his hand and bounced onto the hexagon tiles of his mother's clean bathroom floor. He slid off the toilet and onto the floor, his lips almost kissing the porcelain tub. I thought he was dead.

I heard keys jingle as the front door opened. "Anyone home?" his dad yelled from the foyer. I froze for a second before screaming, "Over here, quick!" Moshe tossed off his coat and pushed past me. After a quick assessment, he said, "He passed out. On heroin?" It was a statement and a question from my future father-in-law that I couldn't answer. Michael's eyes opened in a wide gaze and closed quickly, not out of fright from seeing his dad towering over him, but, as he would later tell me, "from the euphoria of the best high I ever had."

Leaving him lying on the bathroom floor in a content drug-induced stupor, Moshe and I went into the kitchen. Facing one another at the tiny table, he reached out for my hand and said, without looking at me, "Do not marry my son." I chose to ignore his warning, convinced that with my help and love, Michael would simply stop using drugs. It seemed easy enough to do.

That night, Michael and I sat on the plastic-wrapped couch in his parent's living room. Gaining courage from my naiveté, I said firmly, "You must promise me you'll never shoot up again. If you do, I'll leave you." Looking me quietly in the eyes, he promised. I believed that a simple pledge would be enough to erase his demons. And a young woman in love fell into a trance.

So I married my second bellhop on March 28, 1974, just a few days before the hotel was to reopen. Sitting on the living room floor of a friend of Michael's, we said our vows before the local justice of the peace. Looking around for the approval he knew he would get, the justice pulled out a joint as he began our solemn ritual. Michael's friend handed the justice a lighter. He inhaled deeply and then passed the joint to the groom. "Do you take this woman?" The justice inhaled. Filling his lungs with the communal smoke, Michael answered, "I do." And then exhaled.

We went to work the following day, and life quickly took on a routine. I was doing the work expected of me in the office. Michael suddenly was no longer a bellhop. As the new son-in-law, he was promoted to be my dad's assistant, overseeing all the hotel's groundsmen and maintenance men. He also helped run our weekly cocktail parties and any special events at the hotel. It wasn't until years later, when I peeled away the haze of those years, that I realized my dad had quietly and gradually assumed most of Michael's duties.

There were moments of happiness and tenderness between us. Michael was a great storyteller; he would weave tales of feral children hidden away in attics in Northern Wisconsin. Or he told stories about movies he had seen or newspaper articles he had read, his details often more exciting than the real thing. He spoke in a soft voice, and when he told one of his many stories, it was just low enough to make his listeners lean in to hear him.

Winters, we'd sit in front of the brick fireplace in our home, looking out into the forest and fields that surrounded us, watching the trees glisten with their ice-covered branches. Michael would ceremoniously line the arm of our couch with an apple, a pipe, some pot and the remote control. And we would snuggle all evening. In the early years, he was capable of such loving moments as he was of shoving a needle into his veins.

At times he could be an attentive husband and devoted father. He held our daughter just moments after she was born; it was the only time I saw him cry. When she was only a few months old, he'd prop her up on his naked chest, and together they would nap. Often, Jo Anna would say, "No, Mommy, let Daddy comb my hair." And I loved it when she smiled and told me she was off to work with her daddy.

In 1979, when we were married for five years, Michael decided he was going to produce rock concerts. With his feet propped up on his desk, cigarette in hand, he'd sit on the phone for hours, claiming he was talking to associates. When I came into the office, he'd often shush me, implying this call was of the utmost importance. I vaguely listened as he spoke endlessly about his business plans. To whom? I have no idea. That summer he completed erecting the façade of a business executive; his mannerisms changed and his voice deepened. And his distance from me increased.

While he was pretending to be a successful businessman, I was fully engaged in my work, managing the kitchen. Once I became a mother, I had a nanny who also cleaned my home daily. My mother often babysat during dinner. The kitchen staff prepared my food. As a result, I had it much easier than most women had in balancing my work life and being a mother.

However, very often while I was busy working and taking care of our daughter, Michael was nowhere to be found. He was good at masquerading, often making it appear like he had just been there. Or perhaps I just wanted to believe that. Sharing a sense of silent knowing, my dad and I shoved all this separately into our own sacred sewage bins.

"Where were you?" became my mantra. Michael's answers were as varied and creative as he was conniving and shrewd. I feared challenging his answers. Instead, I swallowed his lies, letting them creep deep within me, creating a painful canvas that became increasingly familiar. The veils of the truth of who Michael was and what he was doing were still so thick they blinded me.

I observed his swollen arms and ankles and told myself that was normal. I suppressed my feelings about his disappearances and depression. I was in denial about his nodding head and contracted pupils. I vaguely noticed how he'd wear long-sleeved shirts on hot summer days. I questioned why he undressed and dressed in private. My questions floated in the air, unanswered. I felt abandoned when he stopped making love to me, but still, I preferred to stuff my feelings away into a dark corner.

By now, we fought often. Michael saw me as the yoke holding him back from becoming the next Clive Davis in the rock world. In October of '79, we separated. We had sold our home the previous spring and had been living at the Brickman for the summer. When the hotel closed for the season, my father offered Jo Anna and me the apartment where Grandma had lived. Feeling her presence during that long winter of our separation, I felt nourished by her spirit. Michael spent that winter in Los Angeles with his mother and sister, ostensibly trying to fulfill his dream of being a rock producer. By late February, he was out of money and ready to come home. During those months, I had glimpses of independence, but mostly I felt out of balance as if one of my legs had been amputated and I couldn't find a crutch. I wasn't ready to be alone. As spring approached, I agreed he could come home. I replaced my well-being with expertise in denial.

On a chilly March day in 1980, just a few weeks before our sixth anniversary, Jo Anna, now 2, and I drove to LaGuardia Airport to pick up her dad. She leaped into his arms as he opened the car door, crying, "Daddy, Daddy!" We lived with him for another five years.

Chapter 13

A Family Reunited

The first time I met my cousin, Rita Brickman Domnitz (2001)

One July morning in 1975, I found Grandma in the kitchen, sitting at her table with two large trays of salt and pepper shakers in front of her. She had already filled all the salt shakers and was in the middle of doing the pepper. "I can't stop sneezing!" she told me as she reached for her handkerchief. She had been filling up pepper shakers for as long as I could remember, but now she admitted, "I'm getting too old for this. All this sneezing is making me exhausted." Her smile told me she wasn't ready to give up her job, but she did ask me to walk her home. But by the summer's end, Grandma wasn't able to come to work. I visited her in her apartment almost every day. She would question me extensively, wanting to know all the latest gossip.

In late August, nearly 40 years after the Brickman family fell apart, my dad nonchalantly mentioned to me, "Kate is coming to visit Grandma." I looked at him in disbelief. The key players in my dad's youth, the people who had grown up with him at the hotel, remained elusive to me. The few times he talked about his aunts, uncles or cousins, he always used the past tense. I thought they were all dead.

And now, Kate, the daughter of Jehiel Brickman, my grandmother's oldest brother, was coming to visit. My dad gave me a sheepish smile, which I knew meant it wasn't the time for deeper questioning. "Come with me to tell Grandma."

The name Brickman embraced my life, feeling more like my name than Posner. Even after Grandma shared our family story with me, my dad rarely talked about our family, and Murray had no interest in helping me find my place in this story.

Grandma's room was enormous, cave-like and yet welcoming. At almost 90, she was sitting in bed, looking regal in her satin robe, when we entered. "You look so serious, Benny," she said to my dad. I could tell he was nervous; he was fidgeting with his eyebrow. I sat beside her and asked, "Dad, should I tell her?"

"You're making me nervous. Vat? Vat? Tell me." I loved her accent.

"Mom," my dad began, "Kate, your niece, wants to come to visit you." Those few words made her smile, as I had never seen before. Then she closed her eyes and began to sob, and I gently took her hand. My dad continued, "She is coming next week with her daughter, Renee, and her son, Neil."

"Why, after so many years? Of all my family, it is Kate that I missed the most. We were so close."

"I don't know why now, Mom," my dad answered as he held her hand. "Kate must be in her 70s. Renee? 50-ish."

Just then, the door opened. The three of us turned. No one ever knocked. "Murray, did you hear?" Grandma shouted, sounding like an excited girl. My uncle walked over and knelt beside her.

"Yes, I heard. Mom. I have seen Renee many times." he confessed.

Her smile evaporated. "Murray, what are you saying?" My dad touched his mother's shoulder. I sat there motionless.

"When I would visit travel agents in Washington. She lives in D.C. Years ago, I called her, and she asked me to come over for dinner. So I did." He motioned for me to get up so he could sit next to his mother. I walked over and stood with my dad. He rested his hand on my shoulder.

"We kinda made a tradition of it. Renee has three sons, Eric, Doug and Neil. You'll meet Neil next week."

Leave it to Murray. In the midst of his betrayal of the family, he also was the catalyst for this reunion. "Oy," my grandmother and dad sighed simultaneously.

"Vell, at least I will get to see Kate before I die." And she reached over and hugged Murray.

On the day Kate was to visit, Grandma and I were so nervous as we waited for her to arrive. Finally, the door creaked open.

"Aunt Annie!" Kate cried as she hurried over to my grandmother, giving her a hug and sitting next to her. Renee and Neil stood near Kate, protective of her as I was of my grandmother. Grandma looked from Kate to Renee in evident confusion. "Kate," she said, looking directly at Renee." Renee patiently explained who was who, but Grandma never fully sorted it out. She couldn't grasp that the older woman was Kate.

I saw myself in Kate. My mother was short, 5', with jet-black hair and matching dark eyes. My father and his mother were large-boned. I could never find my face in theirs. Kate and I were about 5'4", with blue eyes and slender bodies. I stared uncomfortably at her for a moment, then smiled. I could now release the fear of being adopted and not being told.

Kate reached tenderly for Grandma and stroked her white hair, their tears mixing with smiles. Renee and I, strangers to one another, stood like sentries over the women we loved as Kate and Grandma talked and hugged and reminisced and cried. Their love for one another was unmistakable. I kept noticing the peculiar expression on Grandma's face — was it utter joy or perhaps sorrow for all the love she had lost?

Grandma entered the hospital two weeks after Kate's visit. I watched her take her last breath on September 7th. We buried her the following day and sat shiva until sunset that evening. The next night was Rosh Hashanah, so our shiva was short. Since there was such strain between my mother and Aunt Helen, having to sit shiva for only a few hours eased much family tension. However, even with the family dynamics, the shiva was full of love, gratitude, stories, tears, food and laughter.

It took another 27 years for the descendants of Molly and Abraham Brickman and Joseph and Anna Posner to meet. In 2002, I received an email from Eric Amrine, Renee's youngest son. Eric and his brothers had fond memories of Murray's visits when they were children. I was the missing piece to make the family whole. Through Eric, I was reunited with all of my Brickman cousins. My dad was still alive when Eric reached out to me, and with evident pride and joy, my dad embraced our entire family.

The first Brickman I met in person was Rita Brickman Domnitz, the daughter of Jess and granddaughter of Jehiel. We planned to meet at a Starbucks in New York City. I was sitting looking out the window, eager to meet her. I saw a woman about my age who looked so much like a Brickman, her curly hair streaked with gray. As she opened the door, I called out to her, "Rita, over here!" as if we were old friends. We sat for hours, two strangers, talking about our grandparents and great-grandparents, Molly and Abraham. On our next visit, I brought all the documents I have from the hotel, the original deeds, stock certificates and dozens of photos. We took ourselves back to the 1920s, when her grandparents, Jeihl and Bryna, came to live at the hotel with her dad, Jess, and his brother, Davie. We traced our shared history, pieced together stories from both sides of our family, and created a framework to tie our family back together.

Eric, the only cousin I have not met, recently saved his brother's life with a stem-cell transplant. Eric flew from his home in Seattle to Brazil, where Doug lived. Doug was in isolation battling his disease, with his partner, Jose, by his side. Four Brickman's cousins, Rita, her sister Jill, Eric and I, exchanged daily emails for that stressful month. We shared laughs, fears, stories and memories. The descendants of Abraham and Molly bonded as Doug successfully fought for his life.

The Brickmans first stepped onto the shores of this country in the early 1900s. They relied on each other to survive and thrive and then came the devastating breakup, the sorrow that sat with my grandmother for decades. Her death was peaceful, perhaps in part because she got to reunite with her beloved niece, the beginning of what turned out to be a family made whole again.

The Boys

Murray at the front desk

Ben and Murray

Ben

Ben and Murray

Brickman Ads

Brickman Ads

Some of Our Staff

Murray (petting Peppy), Chubby Lenz, Solly Gains, Rocky Black, Grandma, Ben, Ned Harvey

Danny Brachman and Solly Gaines
"A station with a vacation"

Larry Strickler, Mel Simons

The Brickman Family

My Parents' Wedding
June 6, 1937
The last photo of the family together

Back Row, L to R: David Brickman, Rose Brickman, Jesse Brickman, Marjorie Brickman, Ben Brickman
Harry Rosen, Kate Rosen, Joseph Brickman, Murray Posner
Center Row, L to R: Bryna Brickman, Anna Posner, Ben and Rae Posner, Joseph Posner, Anna Brickman
Bottom row: Renee Rosen, Allen Brickman, Bebe Posner

Grandma as teenager   Anna and Joe Posner

1928. Anna Posner is at the far left. Joseph Posner and Molly Brickman in the front row, far right. This is the car in the fatal accident in which Jeihl was killed.

Chapter 14

I Quit

The Tarry Brae and East Wings of the Main Building

One morning in late June 1976, I was sitting at my desk in the reservation office. Directly across from me was Sandy, Murray's mistress. I had just booked a couple for the last week of summer and was about to give Lenny Rich the information when Sandy said something snippy to me. We barely spoke; when we did, it was short and to the point. I don't remember the exact words, but I recall the tone, it was curt, demeaning and manipulative. I knew one day she'd come after me. Sandy often made subtly rude comments to many of the staff. And now, it was my turn. I bolted out of my chair.

Murray was in the convention manager's office when this took place. I immediately stormed into Betty's office and told my uncle about my confrontation with his "then some." Everyone in the office heard Sandy's verbal attack, and now they could listen to Murray defend Sandy.

Murray looked up at me, which he had never done during one of our encounters, perhaps because he knew I would not accept his supporting Sandy. He refused to believe Sandy was a disruptive force.

It was always someone else, never her. And now he thought I was the instigator. I stood there for a few moments, absorbing what was happening. I couldn't look at him; I was so hurt and angry. "Go back to work!" he said as if ordering me around would calm me down.

"I quit," I said as I turned around and left him sitting next to Betty. Quitting isn't something I ever expected to do. But I did. As I walked back into the office, everyone skirted their eyes away from me. I couldn't look at them either.

Upset as I was, I felt a sense of pride that I had been the one to tell Murray just how I felt about her, how no one could stand her, including my father, how she was creating tension and a schism in our family business. I also felt sad because this was my family's business. The Brickman was my home. I was walking away from a job that I loved. But I had no choice.

As I was digesting what was happening, I knew for sure this was a premier bulletin. I could almost feel Larry and Shelly's ears tingling. I couldn't wait to tell them what had happened.

Someone must have told my dad because I found him sitting at my desk. His eyes told me to come with him to his private office, which we called the money room because it had a large safe where we kept cash to supply the coffee shop, the Smoke Shop and the bars. As tears streamed down my cheeks, I told him what had happened. I could see the frustration and sadness on his face. I didn't want to disappoint my dad, but I couldn't spend my days in the same office with "that woman," as my mother called her. I could no longer look at my uncle.

My dad and I talked for a long time. As was our custom when solving a problem, we first laid out all the options we could think of. I listened to his suggestions; he listened to my thoughts. We both understood this would be my decision to make. I could not return to work as my dad had wanted. I knew he understood why I had to do this, and he gave me his full support.

Neither of us couldn't imagine me not working at the hotel. My family's business no longer employed me. My father was disgusted with his brother, but his options were limited. They had a business to run; the show must go on.

It was mid-afternoon by the time I steered into the driveway of my home in Woodbourne. We had a full house. By now, my father-in-law, Moshe, was afflicted with ALS, Lou Gehrig's Disease, and was spending the summer with us along with his daughter Marsha and son

Arthur. I told them the story. While they felt terrible for me, they also were happy to have me home for the rest of their visit.

Moshe was a full-time gambler. He was a sweet man, but he was as addicted to gambling as his son was addicted to drugs. When Moshe died the following summer, he left his children a stub from OTB, Off Track Betting, from a recent bet on a horse. He lost.

This was the only summer I ever had off, and I loved it. I got up at whatever time I wanted. I hung around the outdoor pool. I stayed out late, going to many of the shows in the nightclub. Lounging around the pool became my new job. I did all the food shopping for our family, which meant I raided the hotel's kitchen for whatever we needed. My sister-in-law cleaned my house, and my brother-in-law cooked our meals. He was as good a cook as his sister was a housekeeper.

As soon as Marsha graduated college, Bertha, my mother-in-law, divorced Moshe and moved to Los Angeles. Bertha's life was like her closet, neat and orderly; anything brewing within was carefully swept away. Her metal kitchen cabinets echoed her starkness, but the chocolate cookies she baked with their gooey centers told of a softness that she seemed to have neatly folded, tucked so far away it was nearly forgotten.

As the summer waned and we were into the lazy days of August, my dad called me and asked me to come to the hotel. He said we needed to talk. As I walked through the East Wing lobby, I saw him on the shuffleboard courts, staring at the putting green. He smiled when he saw me.

Without saying a word, he put his hand on my shoulder. We walked silently to the coffee shop. I kept thinking, what did he have to tell me that required us to get a milkshake or, better yet, an egg cream?

"Sit down. I'll get us a couple of egg creams." Moments later, as he brought the drinks to our table, I started to relax. He was smiling.

"I have the perfect job for you," he said as he placed the egg creams in front of us.

"I am not going back to work in the office," I was adamant.

He slowly took the wrapper off his straw and placed it in his drink. I knew he wanted to create some drama. So I humored him and let him take a sip before I said, "Will you tell me already?"

"You are going to be the new kitchen manager, the steward,"

With the death of my grandmother and the retirement of Joe, our long time steward, the kitchen's dynamics changed, adding to my father's responsibilities. My dad thought this would be a good opportunity for me. I was not expecting this. I would have to work at least 70 hours a week, seven days a week, for the seven months we were open. It meant presiding over a staff of about 75 men, which included department heads, cooks, porters and the wait staff. Many of our kitchen staff were marginalized by society. Several lacked proper documentation to even be in the U.S.

All I knew about the kitchen was how to sit at the pink-flamingo table and eat, raid the cookie cabinet with my grandmother and appropriate food to bring back to my house. And now I was supposed to run a kitchen that fed hundreds of people three meals a day, every day. For all this, I had only one qualification: I was Ben Posner's daughter. And with that came a certain expectation: to succeed.

My first reaction was fear, but a strange anticipatory sense of excitement soon supplanted that: This would change my life.

As my mother's agoraphobia took over her life, my dad morphed into a combination of mother and father to me. He was the parent who got me up each morning, made me breakfast, drove me to school, helped me with my homework, bought my clothes, and almost all the other things my friends' moms did for and with them. Most nights, when the hotel was closed, he would take me out to dinner, just the two of us. Some of the waitresses in the restaurants thought he must be a widower.

With a shyness laced with tenacity, my dad was the parent who spoke to me about sex. We both looked down at the floor the whole time he spoke. He had no idea how to assist his young daughter develop into a strong independent woman, let alone a sexual woman.

As my dad entered his teen and adult years, he adopted the societal views of women that were the norms of those years. As I entered my adult years, women were on the threshold of feminism and women's rights. As feminism evolved and women were striving for more acknowledgment and position, my dad understood that he needed to expand his own expectations of what women could be and what they could accomplish, given the chance. He began to see that a woman could, perhaps, be the manager of the Hotel Brickman kitchen — and that his daughter was that woman.

And now my father, with whom I already was very close, was going to be my boss and mentor. We both knew we had to make this succeed since I would never return to being a reservation clerk, and there was nowhere else for me to work at the hotel. My dad treated me as a combination of employee and daughter, as he patiently yet firmly guided me in my new job. I found myself, my skills, my humor, my strength, my curse words, my confidence and much of my wisdom. It became my last and best job at the hotel.

Chapter 15

Life at the Pink Table

A week after I was "hired," I walked into the kitchen for my first day as steward. I went over to my dad at the pink table. Suddenly the entire space looked different, unnaturally large. Even the color of the table seemed to have faded. As I sat down, I marveled at how everything looked so familiar and yet strange. I had never paid attention to how large the kitchen was, how long the range was or the number of employees. What I had taken for granted all my life suddenly became something I was asked to manage.

My dad told me my initial task was to sit and observe the process. At first, all I saw was a prolonged rush of activity: waiters racing, busboys schlepping, orders being yelled, food being plated. These were things I had taken notice of all my life, only now I was seeing them with a new perspective. I kept blinking, trying to focus, to get a feel for the pace, the sounds, the smells and the organization of the movement that seemed chaotic in an incongruously patterned way. My dad asked me to make a list of what I thought did and didn't work. My first suggestion was to have the waiters line up in a new configuration as they waited to place their breakfast orders. This proved more efficient when we tried it out the next morning. I was off to a good start.

Within the first few weeks, I rearranged the six walk-in refrigerators and two freezers, each the size of one of our guest bedrooms, and each had been a hodgepodge of boxes. When I was done, the cooks could clearly see what was in them. I also reorganized the downstairs storage room so each kitchen department had its own space. Then I wrote up a spreadsheet to mirror the storage space, so filling the orders took much less time. I discovered that I had a natural talent for organizing. I was beginning to feel at home in the kitchen once again.

But organizing was just one part of the job. I didn't know how to react if I saw a waiter committing some infraction, tossing out some recyclable livestock, or nibbling on a leftover. Being inexperienced and overwhelmed with all my new responsibilities, I stepped into the job with a mix of eagerness, fear and a bad temper. I was at a loss on how to manage the kitchen and my staff, even though I had watched my grandmother and father handle everyone with such ease. I had never seen my dad or Grandma yell at a staff member, but I had witnessed Murray yelling without shame in public at people who worked for him. So who did I emulate at first when reprimanding the staff?

Uncle Murray, I'm sorry to say. I found myself, also in public, unabashedly yelling at waiters for a slight misconduct. Only much later did I realize such behavior was a mask for deep insecurity, whether Murray's or my own.

At the time, however, I could not imagine Murray as an insecure man. He was the co-owner of the hotel, he had a law degree and he appeared every inch a man in control, until he began screaming vulgarities at his key staff members.

As I grappled with this male environment, I realized I needed to figure out how to step into my femininity effectively. My mother offered me glimpses of what she thought a woman should be, but for her, it was all about the externals: your looks and how thin and well-dressed you were. The ultimate objective for me was to find a husband. And now, I had to figure out how to be an effective manager.

My mother didn't have the skills to teach me how to be a wife, a homemaker or a mother, let alone the manager of a kitchen. The housework was done by a chambermaid when we lived at the hotel, and when I was a child by a cleaning lady during the winter months, we lived at home. When the hotel was open, she never had to cook, and when the hotel was closed, my dad made my breakfast and took me out for dinner five nights a week. Occasionally my mother would show up in the dining room at the hotel to greet the guests; she could be quite charming. But for the most part, she was home alone.

She shredded my self-esteem. I never felt good enough, thin enough or pretty enough. After years of her wishing I had a smaller nose, I decided to have a nose job. I was 22. I didn't discuss it with my mother beforehand. But I consulted my dad. As he did with most matters concerning me, he asked why I was doing this, he shared his thoughts and then fully supported my decision.

I remember my mother walking into my hospital room after the surgery. I was sitting in bed, my long hair shielding my face. Bandages covered my new nose; my blue eyes squinted as I looked out at her. As she approached, I sunk into the mattress, afraid of her judgmental gaze. What I felt from my mother was the distance between us — nothing an observer would notice, but just enough for us to take notice.

Because of my mother's emphasis on what she looked like, I have devoted my life to discovering who I am and how to make the world inside of me content, loved, beautiful and confident.

Recently I looked at photos of myself as a teenager. I focused on my face. And what I saw was a beautiful teenager, her face made even more interesting because of the shape of her nose. I wanted to reach into that photo, hug her and tell her that she was beautiful inside and out.

Chapter 16

Consequences

My mom in South Fallsburg, 1940s

"Rae, the government will send us monthly checks for our birthdays this year. For the rest of our lives." My dad thought he was being funny. When my mother looked at him quizzically, he explained that they would be 62 in October of 1976 and could start collecting Social Security. But she seemed uncomfortable with the idea and told him not to bother applying, that they didn't need the money. He was naturally baffled to hear this.

My dad called my Aunt Shirley, my mother's sister, and confronted her with his suspicion that my mother might not be turning 62 that year. After a heated discussion, Shirley finally confessed that my mother and her four siblings had conspired to rearrange their birth order and even where my mother was born, Latvia, not Portsmouth, Virginia, so my mother would be the same age as my father. My aunt still had their immigration papers, which arrived in the mail a week later. After 39 years of marriage, my dad discovered my mother's actual age.

With the Berson family immigration papers in hand, my dad stormed into their apartment at the hotel. He found her in bed and burrowed deeper into the covers than usual. He showed her the piece of paper with her actual birthdate, which meant she was 68, six years his senior. "As if I would have cared. I love you."

He told her to get out of bed and get dressed; they were going for a ride. She blanketed herself deeper in their bed and told him she didn't want to go. "Rae, get dressed," he ordered.

As she slowly dressed, she kept muttering, "They'll deport me, arrest me. You'll divorce me." Her paranoia was rising close to the surface after decades of deception. No amount of time hiding under the covers could have prevented her secret from being unearthed. She must have known this day would come.

As my dad helped her into their car, he told her they were going to the Social Security office to sign up for their benefits. During the ride, she continued to mumble her fears, over and over, until it sounded like one of the spirituals she loved to sing. Once at the office, she stared at the Social Security forms. Her age, 68, glared up at her. Her secret revealed.

Several weeks later, my father found my mother on the bedroom floor, unresponsive. Noticing an empty bottle of sleeping pills on the floor, he reached for the phone and told the switchboard operator to call for an ambulance. Kneeling beside her, he called her name and tried to arouse her, but she didn't react. His face was so close to hers that he could hear her shallow breaths. She faded in and out of consciousness, not responding to his pleas.

My dad called me from the hospital. "Patti." He sounded out of breath. His voice was almost unrecognizable, "Get over here, immediately." He didn't explain. I grabbed the keys to my mother's orange Buick. Fear overtook me as I drove to the hospital, the same one where she had given birth to me.

I met my dad in the hallway, just outside my mother's room. His face was ashen, his eyes swollen and red. He put his arm on my shoulder. I felt its weight. He walked me into the waiting room and motioned for me to sit down. My head was spinning. I welcomed the comfort of the seat. The plastic creaked as I sat down. I almost wanted to laugh.

He started the story slowly, and I grew more frightened with each word. "A few weeks ago, I discovered your mother lied to me when we first met." He paused here for a few seconds, then began again. "Your mother just tried to commit suicide." When he said that word, I gasped out loud. "I found her lying lifeless on the floor in our bedroom." I got up from the sagging couch and walked to the water fountain. Splashing water on my face, I attempted to ease the numbness. I turned to my father, his expression unfamiliar.

I learned that my mother was 68, not 62, that she was born in Latvia, not Virginia. And that my aunt and uncles conspired to help her facilitate this lie by switching their ages so that my mother could be six years younger and the same age as my dad. It was hard to absorb that for a second time my mother had lied to me. And now she wanted to die.

"She'll be OK." my dad tried to assure me. At least physically, I thought to myself. Her mental state was never discussed.

I was 26 and trying to figure out who I was. This was made more complicated by having a mother that I hardly knew. And now I knew she was suicidal. She could be well-dressed, beautiful and charming, but that was just a cover to hide her pain and suffering, her depression and anxiety. And fears. The woman I ached to know was fading even farther away as my dad told me how she deceived him. When he was done telling me this story, we hugged. "We'll get through this," he said. I believed him and felt a moment of reassurance.

My dad offered to go with me to her room, but I wanted to go alone. I wanted to see my mother as much as I feared seeing her. The room was dark, with only a few streaks of light peeking through the Venetian blinds. I saw her silhouetted shape lying there in a fetal position, sliced in half by a shadow draping the room.

She stirred and whispered, "Patti." I wish I could say I walked over to her, took her hands in mine, told her I loved her and comforted her. But I did not. I could not. I did not know how to climb over the brick wall she had been building since before I was born. Instead, I turned and walked out of the room as soon as she said my name.

I felt so alone, not knowing what to do, how to act, not knowing how to be a daughter to my mother. During those times, no one talked about my mother being mentally ill. All I felt was the wall she created, a wall I didn't know how to climb or want to climb. I feared what I would find on the other side. I waited for her to share her story with me. That time never came.

After several days in the hospital, my dad brought her home. In the days that followed, she finally emerged from her bedroom and slowly walked onto her porch. I observed her from afar as she sat down and looked around, pulling her coat tight against her. She did not see me. I wanted to go to her and tell her how sorry I was that I had walked out of her hospital room. I thought about sitting next to her, maybe even holding her hand. But I never did.

"I am sorry." Three words could have brought us closer. I didn't know how to say them, and neither did she. I think she was grateful that I held on to my silence. I watched her and thought back to my childhood when I heard her singing "Amazing Grace."

We never said the word suicide to each other, to her family or to her friends. Occasionally my dad would openly express a desire to leave her, but he never did. That would have meant that the burden of caring for her would fall to me. He understood when I told him I could not be responsible for taking care of her. The thought of being her caregiver made me cringe. I used to secretly fear that my mother would outlive my dad. Ultimately he stayed with her to help me as much as to help her.

Chapter 17

Matzoh Balls and Quaaludes

It's a Tuesday in the summer of 1984. My alarm goes off at 6:30 a.m. I hit the snooze button as I grab more than my share of the sheets and blankets. I roll over, hoping to postpone the start of the day. I slam the snooze button again when it goes off at 6:40. Michael tugs at the sheets just as I'm about to fall back to sleep, and here I am, the sheets haphazardly covering my husband, leaving me exposed with nothing else to do but face the day.

I shower, throw on my clothes and grab my raincoat and umbrella (it's pouring and thundering, a true summer storm). I am out of the door at 7:01. My commute: I back out of the driveway and drive down the hill past the day camp area and the staff quarters. I edge along the guest parking lot (it is full, I notice with an inner nod of satisfaction) and pull into my space in the back of the main building, right beside the kitchen —- the kitchen that I've been running for the last eight years. I enter at 7:05, only five minutes late. But my dad takes notice.

I half expect George, our breakfast chef, to greet me on my way into the kitchen. He usually takes a break at 7:00 to go outside and smoke a cigarette. George is in his early 40s, over six feet tall, with a shiny bald scalp and skin the color of a chocolate brownie.

The back porch, where many of the cooks come out for a break, is a combination receiving deck, garbage dump and hangout. The smell at this early hour is almost sweet. By lunchtime, when the ever-mounting garbage will be hauled away, the only ones left to appreciate the fragrance will be the flies and mosquitoes. Even first thing in the morning, the zapping of the electric fly trap brings me back to the moment. Show time.

Feeding 600 hungry people three times a day is a comedy routine in and of itself. It's like running a circus while herding cats. Part of the tumult is because many of our wait staff and kitchen staff come to work stoned. I have signs all over the kitchen basement that say, "No Pot Smoking Here."

In the early '80s, the drug of choice for our wait staff was Quaaludes, 'ludes for short. Waiters stoned on ludes came in late, dropped dishes and forgot orders. This drug was more for languidly lying by the pool than for participating in the circus we had going on feeding so many guests in just one hour.

One night, Sam, a lover of 'ludes, picked up a tray of 30 steaming hot bowls of matzo ball soup. As he walked past my pink table, he smiled sheepishly at me. He knew that I knew what was making him smile. With that, he melted right there in front of me. Matzoh balls went flying, soup went spraying, and as the last ball hit the floor, so did Sam.

The following year, cocaine became the best friend of my staff. Waiters were in before the crack of dawn to set up their tables, and dishes were brought into the dishwashers at record speed. Not a matzoh ball went flying. Cocaine meshed well with the general frenzy as lox and bagels, brisket, borscht and Danish danced around the dining room tables. Cocaine was now *my* drug of choice — for my staff, that is.

As the steward, I had to come to terms with our staff's drug use. While I was aware that my husband was indulging, I remained in denial about the depth of his addiction. But even had Michael been straight and true, I still would have had to look away when it came to our kitchen and dining room employees. I had a job to do, and if I fired all those who indulged, few would be left and I'd have to replace them with who knows what.

* * *

The screen door shuts behind me and I find myself in the vast expanse of the kitchen. I am greeted by racks holding trays of warm toasty bagels, freshly baked rolls and Danish drenched with fruit. As always, my dad is waiting for me and smiles with a touch of indulgence that says, "I love you, but I'd prefer you show up on time." I smile back and walk past George, who winks at me as he prepares for the onslaught of 20 waiters setting up for breakfast. We have about an hour before most of the 600 guests, plus 75 teenagers, will come charging into the dining room. From the amount of food they will consume just for breakfast, you would think they hadn't eaten since checking in on Sunday. But on this Tuesday, no one has yet missed a meal. Not one.

I open the heavy door of the walk-in refrigerator closest to George. I notice he hasn't taken out the batter he made the night before for pancakes. I make sure there are at least ten cases of eggs handy. He has already taken out the challah French toast on baking sheets ready for the oven. Like many of the staff, George has been with us for several years. His routine is solid.

As George begins cracking a case of eggs, I remind myself to go downstairs to the walk-in refrigerator in the basement to make sure I don't need to order more eggs. We use about 10 cases every week. Each case holds 30 dozen eggs, which translates to 3,600 eggs a week, 15,480 eggs per month and about 108,000 eggs cracked, scrambled, fried or boiled over the span of our seven-month season.

I walk toward my home base, my office, the pink-flamingo table from my grandmother's days in the kitchen. My dad is observing my attention to the early-morning details. I pour my first cup of coffee from a pot on the double burner that is magically refreshed throughout the day from the big urn near the entrance to the dining room. I know that soon the waiters will be in to pick up fresh rolls (plain and onion) and Danish (cheese, prune and plain), all handcrafted by our baker and his staff of three.

* * *

I realized that bakers generally were a bit crazy, at least the ones who worked for us. Maybe it was all the dust from the flour or having to get to work at 4 in the morning. I'm still not sure. I don't bake, nor do I cook. Never had to. For all the years we had the hotel, I had cooks and bakers creating my meals, and today, as I write these words, I have a husband (#3) who is a great cook and baker, and he creates my meals. It feels like home.

As a kid, when Grandma was Queen of the Kitchen, the bakery was my favorite part of the kitchen. It makes me smile to know I have stepped into her space. In those years, and when I ran the kitchen, we produced all our baked goods, Danish and breakfast rolls, and an elaborate array of desserts for lunch and dinner. Challahs were made daily for French Toast, and the ones baked for Friday nights were braided for the Shabbat. There were four dessert choices for lunch and dinner, plus the regulars, cookies, bow ties and something sugar-free. The bakery always had ample buttercream for all the cakes made daily. Dozens of cookies were housed in a cabinet under lock and key because they were so delicious, they had to be protected from being "stolen" as quickly as the baker could make them.

When we were kids, my cousins and I knew that Grandma would get out her precious key to the cookie cabinet when we came into the kitchen. We would drown chocolate chip cookies in buttercream and then top it with another cookie, making a sandwich that still makes my mouth water. Grandma would often admonish us, "That's too much!" but she would invariably pitch in to assist with our creations, helping us decide between chocolate and vanilla for the centerpiece. When all three of us had buttercream dripping down our chins, her face lit up like she was one of us. Then she'd make a sandwich of her own.

* * *

My dad waits for me to get my first cup of coffee, and as I stir in the sugar, he tells me the count for the weekend has risen to 650 and that I need to increase the amount of fish I have to order for Friday night's gefilte fish. On Tuesdays, I order about 200 pounds of pike and carp to be delivered early on Thursday. And since this is a Tuesday, I immediately call Proyect's Fish Market to increase my order.

Chester, our head chef, often will take a pound or two of the fish and shape it into balls, then steam them in a fish broth. Our contractor, electrician and plumber, along with my dad and myself, know to be on time for our special Thursday lunch of gefilte fish soup, all fresh, warm and delicious. Ordering the fish for Friday is so essential to running a kosher kitchen that I often wake up with a start in the early hours of a Wednesday morning, fearful until I reassure myself that yes, indeed, I have remembered to place the order.

With that first cup of coffee, my long day begins. Taking my coffee with me, I walk to the pantry to make sure that the waiters are lining up to pick up their "livestock." I don't mean cattle. Livestock is kitchen jargon for perishable food, most of which comes from the pantry. A half-hour before each meal, the waiters come sauntering into the kitchen, clutching their large silver trays under their arms, ready to pick up their livestock. While on line, all 20 chat about their night at the track, the cutest girl at the teen table or what time to meet at the pool. As their turns come, they each pick up 30 glasses of assorted juice, the livestock and several monkey dishes full of butter and margarine, and several more monkeys loaded with small plastic creamers of half and half. Then they add whatever else they can fit on their trays so that they instantaneously have everything their guests want for breakfast, eliminating making too many trips back to the kitchen.

For the uninitiated, monkey dishes, also kitchen lingo, are small round dishes that have a variety of uses and are often placed on flats. Flats are smaller than lunch or dinner plates. One of their uses is for small portions of the main dish that we refer to as "sides." In addition to a main dish or two, our guests love to order sides (tapas in today's lingo). Sides save us money. Instead of our guests getting two or three mains, we make it cool to have a main and a few sides.

The livestock for lunch is about the same as breakfast, but dinner is slightly different. Breakfast and lunch are traditionally dairy meals, while dinners are meat, so there is no milk or butter with dinner. There is little less livestock to schlep, but dinner is the most intense meal to produce and serve. And it's the meal where the most food goes out to and into our guests.

Eddie, our salad man, presides over long steel shelves lined with flats holding a seemingly endless array of melons, fruits and raw vegetables, ready for the waiters to pick up as needed. They often pick up more than they need, just in case their guests want something extra. Eddie needs at least a case or two of everything from his department every day. Except for melons, of which he uses at least ten cases a day. That's almost 7,000 melons over the course of the summer. Each melon has to be seeded, sliced and plated. As many grapefruits have to be sectioned, multiple salads have to be put together and salad dressing have to be made. Vats of coleslaw are made daily. Barrels of pickles and sour plum tomatoes are prepared in-house and are on the menu every night. Each guest has a glass of juice for breakfast and lunch, a slice of melon at dinner and often at lunch. And at breakfast. Of course, guests can order extra juice or melon for any meal. We encourage them to order as much as they want, and they do!

* * *

The Catskill resorts were much like the all-inclusive resorts that are so popular today. Our guests paid a weekly or daily rate, depending on how long they stayed, which included almost everything except liquor from the bars, food from the coffee shop, sundry incidentals, massages, portraits painted by our resident artist and candy from the Smoke Shop. The rates did not include tips, which is why our wait staff worked so hard to please our guests.

Even though I was the boss and the boss's daughter, I had a friendly relationship with many of the staff. We were all about the same age, and we all had the same goal: to feed the guests, offer good food and service, and then have time for some fun.

* * *

I inspect the dining room, ensuring everyone is ready. The tables are set at each station, the servers are loaded with livestock and the waiters are lounging around for the final few minutes before mealtime begins. After walking the length of the dining room that easily holds over 60 tables, I ease through the swinging doors and back into the kitchen. I walk past the pantry, knowing that Eddie is ready to go.

* * *

For most of the summers I ran the kitchen, we were on a Modified American Plan or MAP, which meant two meals a day instead of the traditional three. We were open later for breakfast and longer for dinner. We did not serve lunch. While the rush at each meal remained the same, MAP gave us all several more hours off in the afternoons, mostly to spend by the pool or playing tennis. Or the unmentionables the staff enjoyed. We jokingly called it a "station with a vacation."

Chapter 18

Breakfast: The Kitchen in Full Gear

Without looking at my watch, I know it is 8 a.m. Time for breakfast to begin. The first half hour is a drip-drip of people coming to eat. By 8:30 the rush starts. George is in ready mode. He has 13 frying pans lined up like soldiers, waiting for the waiters to march in, each with their empty metal tray dangling from their hands. George has two sheet pans full of French toast warming in the oven.

The waiters now have everything they need on their servers. Too much stuff. They have all sorts of goodies to satisfy their guests, which they hope will translate to a bigger tip. They have extra pats of butter sitting on ice cubes, which annoys me. I want everything refrigerated until needed. Still, they sneak so many things out in clever ways to help cut down on their trips to the kitchen. I usually let it go, especially since they provide our guests with quality service. Our waiters are well trained and can handle their guests with professionalism and a certain savvy, making staying at our hotel a memorable Catskill experience.

At 8:30, ten waiters are lined up, and they shout their orders to George one by one. Then a conspicuously older waiter suddenly appears from nowhere and glides to the front of the line, to no one's surprise. It is Solly. Solomon Ginsberg has worked at the Brickman since the mid-1940s. He is one of the many characters who give the hotel its flavor and excellence. When I was two, he gave me a Pollyanna doll that I kept well into adulthood. Solly is charming and has that patented Catskill Mountain savvy dispensed via small talk and kibitzing. His station is at the center of the dining room and is the most prestigious, right near the doors leading into the kitchen. "I'd like to sit at Solly's station." is often heard when veteran guests register. It gives them status, indicating, "I've been here before, I know the routine, I know whom to ask for." While most waiters top out at 30 guests, Solly often has close to 40. Walking around his tables like a mother hen, he caters to his charges with at least seven flats lined up along his arm, a smorgasbord of delicacies on his sleeve.

* * *

One would think he would be remembered for his stellar performance as a waiter, but when I talk to my Brickman friends about Solly, we joke about how he lounged around the pool after lunch with his balls dangling out of his bathing trunks. He evidently had been doing this since he started working at the hotel.

* * *

After Solly picks up his egg orders from George, the other waiters, mostly young men, begin to give their orders; then they are followed by another 10, then another 10. "I'll have two eggs over easy, two cheese omelets, one with onions, three orders of pancakes, and two French toasts." Each waiter rattles off similar orders as George orchestrates his fry pans, whipping out eggs galore. His assistant dishes out French toast while making up to 20 pancakes at a time on the griddle.

The pace is fast, the voices are loud and the meals are delicious. As the waiters pick up their orders, they top each plate with a metal cover. Then, with 10 or 12 mains stacked up, they hoist their full trays high in the air so the tray settles back down atop their splayed fingers.

Each waiter has his own unique technique, adding to the rhythm of the kitchen.

We have only a few waitresses on the staff who have to carry the same amount of food on their trays as their male counterparts. As I watch them lift their heavy trays, waiting an extra moment to find their balance, I feel a sense of pride as they hustle back to their stations. I wish more women worked in our dining room. Each waiter and waitress makes this trip at least three times, one for each table at their station.

I insist that they serve one table at a time. I doubt they like having to do this. If they had their way, they would make only two trips, serving a table and a half at a time. During the dinner meal, especially, I keep a close eye on how many mains they take out each trip. They do their best to sneak out more than one table's food, and often I would look away. While the waiters are getting their hot mains, the busboys are racing back and forth from the dining room with bus boxes full of dirty dishes. They also replenish rolls, Danish, livestock, pickled herring and lox, so their guests don't go hungry. Coffee and tea are served, juice is sipped, Danish nibbled, cream cheese smeared on bagels and then topped off with lox.

As the pace of the kitchen hits full speed, the dishwasher, affectionately called Big Bertha, is chugging away. "Bertha" is at least 10 feet long and operated primarily by two men. Their assistants empty the bus boxes and organize the dishes so the head dishwasher can slide them into the slats on the conveyor belt. On the other end, another man stacks the dishes onto a nearby shelf, and from there, more assistants put the dishes back on their appropriate shelves. By appropriate, I mean separated into meat and dairy to conform to kosher dietary laws. Breakfast and lunch dishes are red-trimmed to signify dairy, while dinner dishes are blue-trimmed for meat. Most of our kitchen and wait staff are not Jewish; many are from Central and South America. They have no idea what kosher means, but they know to keep meat and dairy dishes separate and never to serve meat and dairy at the same meal.

* * *

Until the 1960s, the hotel was open mainly from Memorial Day weekend to Labor Day, and many of our waiters were young Jewish men from New York City. We would host guests on weekends in the spring, which made it ideal for college students to work in our dining room. Their tips helped pay for their college degrees, and many who worked in the dining room went on to medical or law school. As we began to open earlier in the year and stayed open later, we needed a staff that could work from early spring to late fall. By the time I took over, our staff was more diverse. Many of the wait staff were men from South and Central America, and several were older professional waiters; several were gay, several were black. A few were Jewish.

I don't think our guests or our workers realized the commonalities of their status in this country. Whether it was a Jewish guest, a Brazilian waiter, a man from El Salvador mowing the lawn, all were displaced minorities. Some were in this country for a generation or two, some were survivors of the Holocaust, and many fled violence and poverty — all whose lineage signified coming to the United States in search of a better life. Many of our staff were black men and women, descendants of slaves and part of the great migration from the South. Our hotel welcomed them all.

* * *

As breakfast winds down, the busboys bring in the remaining dirty dishes and glasses and place them near Big Bertha. With shirttails now hanging free, the waiters begin returning their unused livestock and start to meander around the kitchen, noshing on leftovers from breakfast. The busboys wash their silverware and glassware in the smaller dishwasher behind Big Bertha.

For one hour straight, George continues his routine until all 20 waiters have fulfilled their orders and our 600 guests are fed. When the last egg is fried, the last omelet flipped, George takes off his apron and heads outside for a breather and a cigarette. By the meal's end, we have served about 400 orders of eggs, from fried to poached to an assortment of omelets. Add to that 100 orders of French toast, another 100 orders of pancakes and untold pounds of lox, both belly and Nova, plus my favorite, pickled herring. There are very few rolls left over because many guests have created sandwiches wrapped up in napkins, a nosh for later (or "falater," as it has come to be known).

The hum of the dishwasher, the clinking of the dishes, the voices shouting orders, the footsteps of the staff — a harmony of sounds, sights and smells, all meshed together two or three times a day, seven days a week for seven months, creating the melody of mealtime. Then suddenly, the clamor ceases. I look at the clock: 10 a.m. Breakfast is over.

Now the waiters and busboys have a break until noon. Many use this time for a much-needed rest, a smoke (of something or other), a dip in the pool or a nap, before heading back around noon to serve lunch.

As soon as I know most of the livestock has been returned to the proper departments, I head downstairs to the storage room to ensure that I have enough canned goods, eggs, frozen foods and other supplies. This room is large and lined with cases of No. 10 cans that supply the kitchen with whatever it needs. There is one section for the pantry, one for the bakery, one for the kitchen and one for ten 100-pound bags of all-purpose flour, five 100-pound bags of white rice and twenty 35-pound cans of cooking oil. We produce everything we serve our guests except rye bread, white bread, pumpernickel and bagels. My order sheets are coordinated to mirror everything lined up so neatly so that the kitchen staff who retrieve the items I check off can do this without needing to be fluent in English.

On Sundays, after breakfast, I go downstairs to the storage room, the quietest place in the kitchen, and re-energize as I prepare the main order for the upcoming week. I order several hundred pounds of flour and rice and at least 100 cases of food, from sliced peaches to canned tomatoes. The kitchen's expenses comprise about 17 percent of the hotel's budget. This does not include salaries. And even though the chef is our highest-paid employee, there are many weeks when our waiters make even more in tips.

After I make sure my orders are complete, I find my way back to my table and pour myself another cup of coffee — time to take a break until noon.

Chapter 19

Finding My Niche — and My Voice

Me and my dad

I sit for a bit to unwind and sip my coffee. I like taking in the expanse of the kitchen when it's quiet. Then I walk to the lobby, habitually picking up the odd piece of paper that someone has left on the floor. Often I will stop to visit with our resident artist, Joe Hing Lowe, who occupies a corner of the lobby where he does his art. I love Joe and his art.

Joe found his way to the Catskills as an immigrant from China. He was one of the wonderful people who have been at the hotel since I was a kid. I glance at the wall behind him to admire the painting of Karyn and Marcy Strickler, done years before when they were still little girls. Identical twins, they were two years old in 1965 when their father, Larry Strickler, began working as our director of activities.

After a short chat with Joe, I go to the office to see the headcount for the upcoming weekend. Most of our guests come for a whole week, from Sunday dinner through the following Sunday. Several check out on Friday as per the midweek special, leaving us room to fill up again for the weekend.

For most of the history of the Brickman we served three meals a day during the summer months. During the last years of our ownership of the hotel, we were on the Modified American Plan, serving breakfast till 11:30 and dinner. During the rest of the time we were open, we served breakfast, lunch and dinner.

After I get the guest count from Lenny Rich, the reservation manager, I stroll around the property to clear my head for the next meal. I enjoy this time after breakfast when I often run into staff members. We chat as friends. I love it when they can get past me being the boss's daughter. But I enjoy the status and privileges it affords me.

As I walk past the shuffleboard courts, I glance over to the bridge that stretches across the road to our property on the other side. Before the bridge was built in the early 1960s, guests had to cross the road, being careful of approaching cars. Sometime in the 1940s, a guest was run over and killed, which was when the idea of a bridge began.

On the other side of the property are the nightclub, various ball fields, nine tennis courts, the stable, a corral and trails for horseback riding. Several staff buildings also are there, housing the musicians and coffee shop staff. Some raucous times are had in these buildings. I've heard tales of sex and drugs. I remember being told that one of the members of the Latin band climbed out of his room, naked, onto the fire escape as he made his way to another room. I didn't have to ask why. These are stories of young men and women having the time of their lives in the Catskills.

* * *

Even at a young age, I was aware that our staff had good times and that I had an unusual and extraordinary cast of characters in my life. As an adult, I didn't, couldn't know it all, but I had a good idea who was screwing whom, who was stoned and who was gambling away their earnings. It was summer, and many were young and away from home in an atmosphere of freedom. It was a time of coming of age for many. It was the Catskills. Most everyone worked hard and played hard. The fortunate ones went home to their families after the summer or off to college with enough money to pay their tuition. Many of the people of color on our staff went back south for the winter. Others, who came from South and Central America, were intent on sending their earnings back to their families so that they could survive.

We provided room and board for all the staff who wanted and needed it. Their accommodations varied from permanent trailer homes for two of our year-round staff and their families to rooms with a bathroom, to rooms with a shared bathroom down the hall. The wait staff had their own building, where I am sure plenty of partying was happening. The Valley Cottage, on the "other" side of the road, dated back to the early days and still retained its rustic character. Our key personnel had better accommodations than the porters, pot washers and dishwashers, but everyone had a room and three meals a day.

* * *

After I walk by the bridge, I find myself on the top terrace of our pool. I enjoy standing here, watching our guests sunbathe or swim. The Latin band is playing, and many guests are swaying to the beat. Larry Strickler is due to lead a dance class at 11 a.m.

Getting out of the kitchen and walking around the hotel reminds me that we have actual guests who love our nightly shows and enjoy our facilities and our food. In the kitchen, it gets so intense you could forget all this. The emphasis is on producing a meal, and once it leaves the kitchen, it is on to the next meal. I often have to remind the kitchen staff to plate each dish carefully, knowing they never get to see how much their work pleases our guests. What they know is that if we have 600 people, we need enough food to feed at least 800. Maybe more.

Several stone terraces surround the outdoor pool, each lined neatly with lounge chairs. I spot four women playing mahjong in the farthest corner in the shade. (Back then, I wondered what the attraction was to that game. Now, 40 years later, I know.) Finally, I turn to head back to work. I still have a half hour to enjoy a quiet time and catch up on paperwork before the staff returns for lunch.

On my way to the kitchen, I notice the indoor pool is empty, which makes sense. It is a glorious summer day. I don't have much time to indulge in the luxuries our hotel offers our guests, but I do enjoy the pool and an occasional show in the nightclub. I love my job; it is perfectly suited for me. Once I gathered the wait staff together and we talked about how to create a fun and friendly work culture. And we did. My job also allows me to use my organizational skills. I take great pride in knowing I have streamlined this vast adventure into a smooth and efficient routine.

As I push open the door to the kitchen, the familiar conglomeration of scents tells me I am home. Once again, as with nearly every time I enter the kitchen, I am flooded with memories of Grandma.

* * *

We spent so much time here together. She always wore a white chef's apron tied securely around her thick waist, her large breasts peeping out the sides. Her apron was stained from the many times she wiped her wrinkled hands across her belly. She was soft-spoken, yet everyone paid attention to her wisdom and her humor. She had a confident way about her, perhaps from having three brothers. Or maybe because it was she and not any of her brothers that became the owner of the hotel.

As soon as she heard me enter the kitchen, she'd turn to me and smile, creating a web of soft creases around her mouth. She would motion to me to come and sit next to her at her table. If she wasn't at the table, I knew to walk over to the pantry, where I'd often find all five feet of her looking up at Abe, the pantry man in her day. If she was pointing at him, I knew she was reprimanding him, usually concerning livestock that wasn't recycled. But he knew her spiel by heart, having heard it often over the fifteen or so years that he had worked at the hotel. He took it in stride. As a waiter walked by, she was apt to say something like, "Vat, no juice to bring back? Bring in your livestock!" Her tone was far from the grandmotherly timbre she used with me, but her soft Yiddish accent added a touch of sweetness to her statement. When she wasn't hocking Abe over something, they often played canasta at the pink table in the kitchen between meals.

If Grandma wasn't in the pantry I would go to the bakery to look for her. She was just as diligent here with her self-imposed responsibility of salvaging uneaten food, but her tone was lighter as she delighted in seeing cold apple strudel, chocolate cake with dented icing and broken mandelbrot being returned to the bakery. Often, while Grandma thought no one was looking, she picked delicately at a lone linzer tart or a dimpled Danish. When I'd catch her, she'd give me a big grin, reminding me that once she had been young. Then I'd run over to her, knowing she would offer me my favorite, a soft chocolate chip cookie.

Grandma's dedication to the preservation of bread delighted me the most. After each meal, waiters returned any uneaten bread, as they did with the livestock. Her fanciful way of redistributing the bread began with giving the loaves a makeover via her prized possession, the commercial bread slicer that stood right behind the pink table. I giggled when she reshaped loaves of seeded rye, dark brown pumpernickel or braided challah. She had a natural talent for this. She could reshape slices of bread into lopsided but complete looking loaves, almost good enough to serve. Then, she covered her reformed loaves with a clean dish towel to preserve a modicum of freshness. She was also attempting to hide the bread from the head chef, who coveted it for stuffing Friday night's succulent roasted chickens or Saturday night's browned breasts of veal.

My father found his mother's stinginess exasperating, embarrassing and unnecessary. Many times when he saw his mother declaring the urgent need for lukewarm milk or shapeless pats of oleo to be rushed back to the pantry, he cringed. If he caught her saving partially consumed tomato juice, he would immediately pour it down the drain; she'd look at him sideways and be off to find another food that needed rescuing.

"Mom, what are you doing? I could get fined by the Health Department!" he'd argue, knowing it fell on deaf ears. "Vat do *they* know?" she'd contest. "You think you're so rich you can just throw out food? *Vos fa a bullshit is dis?*" Once she started speaking Yiddish, game over.

Yet, when she wasn't looking, my dad would smile at Abe in a way that said, "Go ahead and toss out any questionable food."

When my dad was in his 90s, he needed to take an expensive medication. He decided that he would not spend that much money on a drug. I desperately tried to convince him that not only could he afford it, but he also *needed* this drug. When I told him that he was reminding me of the stinginess of his mother, he abruptly decided to pay for the drug.

To the end, my grandmother was the matriarch, a role she loved. On Monday mornings, after breakfast, Larry Strickler invited guests to join his walking tour of the hotel, always ending it under the family portraits that graced the lobby: a painting of my great grandparents and, directly below that, my grandparents. At noon, you could count on my grandmother to walk by her portrait nonchalantly just as the tour was about to end. "Mama, fancy meeting you here!" Larry would exclaim. "Why, Larry, you must be on your walking tour!" Grandma would reply, always in the same surprised tone. As many of the guests introduced themselves or asked her questions, you could see the joy she took in her unique role in the family business.

Chapter 20

A Humbling Moment

Re-energized from my break, I am ready for lunch. The kitchen is revving up again, and as I enter, the roast cook is preparing hundreds of orders of filet of sole, a lunch favorite. Serving food at a hotel our size always involves planning and preparing in advance. The breakfast cook is already cracking several cases of eggs for tomorrow morning. The baker pulls ten loaves of challah from his ovens for tomorrow's French toast. On Fridays, he prepares forty loaves of challah for the Shabbat dinner.

My dad is sitting at the pink table when I come back to work. I join him for a cup of coffee. We sit for a while, talking about the kitchen, the family and how cute my little girl is.

The kitchen is running smoothly. I am feeling good about myself and the job I am doing. It is all working for me. And out of the blue, my dad sighs wistfully, "If I only had a son."

"Dad," I say in sudden disbelief, "what more could a son do for you?"

He immediately realizes how stupid and hurtful his comment was. He hugs me as soon as we are able to look at one another. This will prove to be a turning point for him and for me.

Not long after his unbelievable comment, I walk into the kitchen as two workers are about to come to blows. The chef sees me enter and motions for me to deal with it. I step right in between these two large men who have worked for me for several years. Sheepishly they walk away. My first thought is, could a son have done any better? I successfully deterred them with the relationship I have developed with them, my managerial skills and my rank.

My mind now shifts to what I need to do to get the orders ready for tomorrow. Each day around 12:30, I go to the chef, baker and pantryman to see what they need for the next day that I haven't thought of. After I talk to the department heads, I go downstairs to check my inventory. Downstairs is an enormous freezer where we keep all the food made in the spring and served during the summer and fall months. Throughout the spring, between breakfast and lunch, the cooks prepare enough stuffed cabbage, egg rolls, kreplach and pierogi for the entire time the hotel is open. That's about 9,000 stuffed cabbages, 9,000 egg rolls, 6,000 kreplach and 6,000 pierogi. Then they are all placed in empty egg crates, sealed and labeled. Once I completed my order, I call our suppliers and place the order, which they deliver early the next day, right in the middle of breakfast.

When I go back upstairs, the kitchen is buzzing. The waiters pick up their lunch necessities, including lemon wedges, glasses of tomato juice, thick slices of casaba melons, honeydew or cantaloupe, squares of margarine and matching pats of butter: livestock. The busboys are loading their bus boxes with enough monkeys and flats for their station.

A half-hour later, at 1 p.m., our 600 guests are waiting impatiently at the dining room doors. The doors open as soon as the announcement, "The Dining Room is open. Lunch is now being served," comes over the loudspeakers, and our guests rush to their tables. They immediately start to nibble on the pumpernickel and rye bread set out for them. Our guests also help themselves to our homemade pickles while the waiters take their soup orders. After the juice, melon, salad and soup are served, the mad rush begins for hot and cold mains. Once again, the waiters fidget with their trays while waiting on line until it is their turn to call out their orders to the cooks.

As part of a busboy's "side job," about 800 plates, in stacks thirty high, have been placed in front of the three serving stations. "I need eight orders of fish, two orders of lasagna and five sides of kasha varnishkes," Ron shouts to the cook as he steps up to the range. He has already picked up a few tuna platters and several glasses of fruit soup. When his order is complete, Ron flings the heavy food-laden tray in the air and onto his fingertips in one smooth move.

The waiter behind Ron, Bruce, shouts a similar order, as do all the other waiters when it comes their turn. It is much more challenging for our waitresses to fling the heavy trays onto their fingers. I watch them with awe as they appraise their trays and bend slightly to lift them off the range and onto their fingers like their male counterparts. Then they hustle out of the kitchen.

Our chef, Chester, is the single most important member of our staff. He is the best chef we've ever had. No one could replace him. Chefs who prepare kosher meals with Chester's expertise are rare. The attention I pay to him has to be subtle, less like a boss and more like a friend. He and his staff of four cooks, two prep cooks and a few helpers are responsible for preparing our lunches and dinners. He gives the Brickman its reputation as the hotel with the best kosher food in the mountains. After all, the Catskills are known for two things: comedy and food: Jackie Mason and roast chicken.

Lunch goes fast, from melon to dessert. Everyone is fed by 2 p.m., including the staff in the staff dining room, who have the same menu as our guests. We have other dining rooms as well, one for the guest children and one for guest infants. And one for our laborers. Although they are treated with respect, in many ways they are isolated from the rest of the staff.

Chester, as well as the roast cook and several other cooks, porters and pot washers start their day at 6:00 a.m. So does George, the breakfast chef, and his assistant. While George is busy with breakfast, Chester and his crew are preparing lunch and dinner in another part of the kitchen. Once all the hot main dishes for lunch have been served, the cooks begin leaving the kitchen. They have one more meal to serve and will be back to work around 5 p.m.; although dinner is already prepared for the most part, they still have another few hours of work. The pot washers and porters work until the pots are washed and the kitchen cleaned. The kitchen is in motion from 6:00 a.m. to about 8:30 p.m., with some off time between meals.

I know if I go to the back porch after lunch, the sweet smell of morning will now be replaced with the stench of garbage. But some of the cooks and waiters wander out anyway to chew the fat and relax with a cigarette.

I usually have my lunch when the meal is being served, but there are days I prefer to sit in the quiet between meals and eat while I finish up some details. The pantryman, on this day, makes me a salad, and one of the cooks has saved me some kasha varnishkes. With the cooks gone, the sounds of the dishwasher become center stage. When Jo Anna was just a month old, I brought her to work. When the dishwasher started its rhythmic tones, she would instantly fall asleep.

* * *

There was one particular moment in the kitchen that transformed me. It was during the summer of 1977, my first full year as steward. I had some details to finish up and decided to do them after lunch was served. As I was relaxing in the quiet of the kitchen and savoring my lunch, prepared by our chefs, I glanced over to the far end of the kitchen, near the bakery, and eyed a stranger. The way he sauntered around disturbed me. His unsteady gait complimented his unwashed Levis and faded sleeveless shirt. A do-rag covered streaks of gray in his wiry black hair. He walked over to the bain-marie near the rear entrance and was just about to spoon leftover meatloaf onto his plate. I motioned to James, a young black man who had worked for us for several seasons, to come over to my desk. He wore a heavy black apron tied around his ample waist that just about reached the top of his worn sneakers. He came to work for us from an employment agency that provided our kitchen with many of our workers. The owner of this agency, the Dependable Agency, scoured the streets of the Bowery in lower Manhattan and filled his van with men on the streets looking for work. James was one of these men, initially hired as a pot washer. This year he was the head dishwasher.

James walked up to me, smiling. "What's up, Patti?"

"Please ask that man, that bum with the do-rag, to put down his plate and leave. He does not work here."

James glanced over at the "bum" and then looked again at me carefully as he searched for the right words to say to his boss.

"I will, Patti. I will ask him to leave when he finishes his lunch." With that, he turned around and walked back to the dishwasher he had so skillfully orchestrated.

As I finished my lunch, I saw James go to the bakery. He placed a few cookies in a paper napkin and wrapped them carefully. Then, James walked over to the man and handed him the cookies. And then he told him he had to leave.

His words, "I will when he finishes," pierced through my elitist arrogance, vaulted past my boss' daughter status, meandered around my middle-class upbringing and white privilege, stopped for a minute to play with my inexperience and landed in a place unfamiliar to me. I have never forgotten James or the man. I wish I knew his name.

This was a transformative moment for me. I was, and I still am, spoiled. I grew up in a resort hotel with cooks, a chef and menus. I never had to think about where my next meal was coming from; it came from the hotel's kitchen. My choices were endless. I had asked the salad man to make me my favorite salad on this day. And he did. I was the boss's daughter, and saying no to me was not on the menu.

But it wasn't until James said, "I will when he finishes his lunch," that something inside me shifted. James knew what it was like to not have the security that I had. My eyes were opened. James' life experience taught him compassion and generosity. This moment humbled me. James' struggles allowed him to understand the plight of the man in my kitchen, which eluded me until James became my teacher. I began to realize that much of who we are comes from our life experiences, circumstances and cultures. But in different ways than I had imagined.

Many of our middle-class guests complained that their steak was too well done or too rare, their soup was too hot or too cold, while perhaps the person who served that steak or soup was sending their hard-earned tips back to families in dire need. During the 1950s and '60s, many young black men worked in our kitchen, cleaned our rooms, swept our floors and helped prepare our meals. During the winter, they went home, many to the deep South. Each year, a few weeks before returning to work, my dad would send them money to make the long drive back, which they had to do in one sweep because few, if any, motels welcomed blacks.

I gained a fresh appreciation for their ability to endure, transcend and transform the burdens they had to bear in our society. Many found comfort in drugs or drink, but they, too, taught me not to judge. We also had several young gay men during my tenure in the kitchen. They added joy to the routine, and their bravery and determination to be authentic was inspiring. I hope they felt a sense of freedom in our hotel. It is tragic beyond words that most of them, as I recently learned, died from AIDS.

Chapter 21

Drama in the Dining Room

Jacinto Loarca usually stayed later than I did after each meal. Among all his other responsibilities, he made sure the refrigerators, freezers, bakery and pantry were locked up when the kitchen was empty. Jacinto helped recruit workers, and he was the translator. He was crucial to the running of the kitchen.

My dad saw something special in Jacinto when he found his way to the hotel from Guatemala in 1966. He was given a year-round job, which was offered only to a special few, our winter staff never exceeding five. A year or two later, his wife, Violetta, came to work for one season. Their five young children stayed in Guatemala while their parents worked hard to support their family. During the winter months, Jacinto had a room near Grandma's apartment with access to her kitchen. One evening in late December, when I visited Grandma, I heard him sobbing. I walked to the other end of the apartment to give him his privacy. I could feel his loneliness.

On February 2, 1976, a major earthquake hit Guatemala. Four days passed, and Jacinto still had not received any news about his family. Then, on the fifth day, Violeta finally got a call through to the hotel. My dad answered the phone, and upon hearing her voice immediately handed it to Jacinto. His face grew ashen as he learned the news of his family: They were all alive but in a terrible situation. They had lost everything. My father immediately asked Jacinto what he could do to help.

A week later, there they were. Violetta and their five children, Fernando, Julio, Caesar, Dora and Alcira, were standing in front of the Main Building in clothes for a much warmer climate. Just days after they arrived, my dad, who was president of the local school board, gathered up his "new grandchildren" and marched them into school. Today, each Loarca child has a master's degree, but on this first day, they were scared little children entering a new world and having to learn a new language.

Happily, nothing could have better prepared them for the future than the stern but loving parenting that Violetta and Jacinto provided them, along with considerable guidance and support from my family. Violetta became the staff waitress, and once each child turned 15, they started working in her dining room, and several graduated to the main dining room. Jacinto and I worked side by side, running the kitchen for many years. He helped me succeed in my job.

My father provided a home for the Loarcas across the street from my house. Within a few years, with my dad's sponsorship, they all became citizens of the United States. To this day, they are my family.

Years after we sold the hotel when I was living in Florida, I got a call from Dora. She wanted to come for a visit. "Which airport should we fly into?" she asked. "Either West Palm Beach or Fort Lauderdale," I told her. She went on to explain that she and her husband had their own plane and wondered if there was an airport near us they could fly into. I had no idea. I pictured Dora as a young girl eager to figure out her new life in America. I was so proud of her and her whole family for creating successful and happy lives for themselves.

When we sold the hotel, one of the hardest things my father had to do was tell the Loarcas they would have to leave the only home they had known in their new country. But, resilient as always, they bought a property a mile from the Brickman with two houses on it, one for themselves and one to rent. The Loarcas genuinely embody the American Dream.

* * *

One summer day after lunch, I stayed late in the kitchen so Jacinto could go with Violetta on some errands. Sitting in that kitchen alone, I got antsy, so I strolled into the dining room. The guests had all left to go to the pool, play golf or tennis, take an art class, listen to a lecture, play cards or mahjong.

Mel Friedman, the maitre d', was standing in front of the closet at the dining room entrance. When he heard me, he turned around. His face was white and he looked unsteady. I helped him sit down.

I was about to pick up the phone and ask for assistance when Sandy, my nemesis, walked into the dining room. This was not the time for hostilities. She stayed with Mel as I called for a bellhop to bring a car to the back door of the dining room. Slowly we got Mel to his feet and helped him walk to the waiting car. The bellhop helped us get Mel into the back seat. Sandy sat next to Mel, and I drove to the emergency room.

Mel managed to tell us that his wife was playing cards by the pool at the Pines Hotel. I promised him I would contact her and get her to the hospital as soon as possible. As they eased Mel onto a stretcher and rolled him into the ER, I told Sandy to stay with him while I called his wife.

I told the switchboard operator at the Pines who I was and why it was urgent that she page Mrs. Friedman. I waited anxiously for about 15 minutes before Mel's wife finally got on the phone. She sounded annoyed. I told her what had just transpired and that I would arrange to have someone from the Brickman pick her up and bring her to the hospital. "No," she said. I didn't get what she meant and started to repeat what I had just told her when she simply said, "I understand," and hung up. Was she more concerned with finishing her card game than her husband's life?

When I returned to the ER, Mel looked listless and had deteriorated while I was gone. As I whispered to Sandy about my experience with Mel's wife, a nurse said they had to take Mel to the OR for emergency surgery. I will never forget the look he gave me as they rolled him out, a look that said, "I know I'm going to die." And indeed, he passed away mere minutes later before they could get him into surgery.

I felt ashamed for him. He passed away without a loved one at his side. I didn't understand it then or now. After we got back to the hotel, I looked into his closet by the dining room and found all sorts of pill bottles. I was thankful I did not run into his wife when she finally returned to the hotel. It wouldn't have been pretty.

Having to share this difficult time with Sandy challenged me. We had barely said a word on the way to the hospital, with Mel our primary focus. However, we shed our defensive personas on the ride home. We compared notes on how hard and unsettling these last hours had been for us, especially with his wife refusing to come and be at her husband's side. It was nice to see a more compassionate side to Sandy.

But as soon as we were back at the hotel, we slipped back into our accustomed mutual antagonism.

Chapter 22

Life Between Meals

Jo Anna and me, 1979

On a day when our maitre D' *isn't* dying, I have a few hours to myself between lunch and dinner. I first go home to change my clothes, which have taken on the dual fragrance of pastrami and pot roast. Then I head over to the day camp to check on Jo Anna.

Our camp starts at 9 a.m. with breakfast in the children's dining room, where our guests drop off their children so they can dine in the main dining room. Camp runs until 5 p.m., then resumes at 6 for dinner so parents can enjoy their dinner on their own.

Few parents opt out of having their kids in day camp because it allows them to enjoy all the hotel activities while knowing their children are well taken care of and having a great time. Many weeks we have up to 100 children in the camp.

As I approach the camp, I figure Jo Anna will want to stay there and not hang with me, even if I tempt her with a visit to the outdoor pool. Indeed, when I walk into the camp house, she sees me and hides behind another child, hoping I won't see her. They are rehearsing for a play they will perform for parents on Saturday. I understand the excitement. I loved performing on our little outdoor stage when I was a camper.

Going back outside, I sit on the swings remembering my days spinning on the carousel, climbing on the monkey bars and swimming in the day camp pool. I walk over to the sandbox and run my fingers in the sand. Jo Anna suddenly appears at my side: "Mommy, Mommy, I want to stay here. I'll see you later." I toss some sand her way and tell her, "See you later." She kisses me and runs back to her group. I am so happy that Jo Anna has the experience of living in a resort hotel.

As she runs off, it occurs to me that I haven't seen her dad all day, and by this point in our marriage, I no longer care. He takes care of Jo in the morning, getting her ready for camp or school, depending on the season. The first morning he had full responsibility for our young daughter, he called me at work. He sounded frantic. I was so scared that something had happened to her in the hour I had left the two of them alone. "You didn't leave any clothes out for her," he screamed at me. The kitchen was in full noisy swing, and he wanted to know what to do about dressing his child. "Pretend I'm dead!" I yelled and slammed down the phone. Yet, I also was relieved that nothing terrible had happened to her due to carelessness from his getting high. Facing the fact that he was a full-blown drug addict was still off in the distance.

With the afternoon to myself, I go back to my house, which borders the camp's ball field. I stand by my living room window looking out at the field and the trees surrounding it, and once again feel blessed. In the summer, kids play soccer or baseball there; during the off-season, the staff has soccer matches. Winter is a special time when the fields and the woods are filled with crystalline snow, and deer come up to nibble on our salt block as the wind sings its song.

My house is nice and quiet. I'm not in the mood for a nap, so I put on my bathing suit and head down to the outdoor pool. I know half the dining room staff will be there, and I am comfortable being their friend in such a carefree environment. At work, I transform back into their boss.

All the lounge chairs on the terraces surrounding the pool are taken. The sun is shining, and several couples are dancing to the mambo band playing on the stage near the shallow end of the pool; Larry Strickler is singing. When the band takes a break, Larry begins a round of "Simon Says" and soon draws a group of thirty happy participants.

I find an empty lounge chair next to Rochelle Kovar, our dining room captain, in the staff area on the top terrace. "Buy me a drink," she says just as I'm getting comfortable. I am entitled to "buy" things for anyone I want to treat. I like this part of being a Posner.

Though they are all staff, Rochelle, Larry, Shelly and our master of ceremonies Mel Simons are my dear friends. One evening we were all in the coffee shop and ordered lots of food, my treat. We were laughing and gossiping about the guests and staff. It was getting late. I had to get up earlier for work the next day than they did, so I excused myself before the night was over and went home. The next day they cornered me, teasing me that I had forgotten to pick up the tab (as in pay for everything). They had to pay the bill, which included my BLT. We all burst out laughing.

Rochelle and I notice Shelly watching her husband, Larry, doing Simon Sez and wave to her, which she knows means, "come join us for an afternoon drink." As she meets up with us, we do our routine of "Did you see Solly's balls?" giggling like little girls.

As we sit down, the bartender places three mimosas in front of us. He had seen us coming. While we sipped our drinks, several guests stand in the pool's shallow end, talking and laughing. Others are on the steps. Shelly, Rochelle and I fall into a spirited gossip session. The time flies by, and already it is close to 4 p.m. "I gotta go," I say, with just an hour to get ready for dinner and pick up Jo at camp. I make sure to sign the tab.

My house is empty when I return home. I quickly shower and change, then set out to get Jo Anna. As always, I love watching the campers come traipsing down the hill from the day camp to the area just outside the indoor pool. Most of the kids walk in pairs, holding hands and singing the songs they've been practicing in camp. Jo Anna is at her customary place at the end of the line, on her own, looking around at the flowers and all her favorite places. When she spots me, she runs over. I lift her and spin her around.

"Can I come to work with you?" she pleads with yearning blue eyes, knowing I can't say no. She especially wants to work with Violetta. She grabs my hand and leads me up the ramp to the kitchen. As if on cue, we both say "P.U.!" at the stench from the garbage at the back entrance.

My daughter has been coming to work with me since she was one month old. As an infant, she loved having so many faces smiling at her while she sat in her little seat, propped up on my pink table. The chef would come over and entertain her whenever I got up to do something.

Jo Anna lets go of my hand as we enter the kitchen. She glances over at the bakery, but no cookies are lying around. She automatically looks for Violetta. She is impatient to go to work, which she has been doing since she was five. Violetta smiles at Jo and motions for her to come with her to the staff dining room. A few minutes later, I poke my head in, and my little girl is carefully placing dinner plates at each setting. I love knowing how at home she is at the hotel and how independent she is among our staff and guests.

After the night session of camp, she will come into the kitchen to meet me. On the nights the rock and roll band plays at the pool, she'll ask if she can listen to the music. I always say yes, and off she'll go, by herself, to the outdoor pool. She knows to meet me in the office at 9 p.m. The hotel is such a safe environment. We offer parents a "night patrol" option so that, when they are at the show in the nightclub, a staff member goes to their room to check on their sleeping children.

The waiters start strolling in around 5:30 for dinner. I notice Bruce, one of my favorite waiters, walking in with his arm around the waist of Annie, one of our waitresses. Another summer romance. He started as her busboy and ended up her husband.

* * *

Every year love simmered with the hot summer sun. A hot night, a lust-filled week, a lifetime together. From my grandparents down through the generations to me, many of us met our spouses at the Hotel Brickman. I hope most of the young people, staff and guests who found love at the hotel hold their memories of the time they shared in the mountains dear.

As much as love was a summer theme, so was death.

In the middle of one show, the female singer asked two men to join her on stage. The crowd laughed and applauded as they clumsily leaped onto the stage like two heroes. As they sat on the two chairs placed on either side of her, she crooned a sweet, sexy love song. Midway through the tune, the man on the left keeled over, dead. That qualified as a showstopper.

On another occasion, I saw a woman guest running frantically from her room in the Ranch House shouting, "Henry, Henry, he's dead! He's dead!" It turned out that in a moment of passion, Henry's heart gave out. Uncle Murray heard the screaming. He ran to get an ambulance as I escorted the distraught woman back to her room. When told that room 310 would be checking out early, our no-nonsense reservation manager, Lenny, simply said, "Oh good, I need the room. We're overbooked."

These things happened, love, sex, laughter and death, when you dealt with almost 20,00 people over seven months our hotel was open. Life went on. As did dinner.

Chapter 23

My Friend Jose

Waiters picking up "livestock"

After a few years of mentoring and training me, my father stepped away from most of his responsibilities in the kitchen. I was ready, and so was he. He still came into the kitchen daily and had all his meals there, but he rarely got involved with the daily operation. However, he continued to do the ordering from Kessler's Butcher Shop, which meant our hotel's butcher, Jose Castillo, answered to him more than to me.

At Kessler's, my dad picked beef sides that Jose would cut up into steaks, roasts, briskets and stew meat. I had gone on some of these runs with my father, but I never quite got the hang of going through those vast, bone-chilling walk-in refrigerators. I had to contort my body as we walked through the maze of cow body parts dangling precariously from the ceiling. I couldn't help noting that they would be on our menu. I was glad my dad never relinquished ordering from Kesslers.

Jose was my best friend at work. His day started early, around 6 a.m. He needed to get his supply of meat ready for the chef by 7, so the cooks could begin preparing for dinner. By the time I came to work at 7:05, depending on the day, roast beefs would be roasting, steaks searing, briskets braising and, for sure, chickens roasting. These smells dominated the kitchen.

During my first full season working as steward in 1977, I was pregnant. Morning sickness was a staple of my life. Most mornings, I could make it to work by 7:05 without having to throw up. Many mornings when I walked in, the steaks were sizzling, roast beef was roasting. Immediately I made a beeline past my dad and Jose to get to the ladies' room, which was nowhere near the kitchen. I knew I would get some teasing and sweet attention when I returned. When I sat next to Jose, my dad would pour me a cup of coffee. And my day would begin.

Jose and I worked side by side for ten years. For the seven months the hotel was open, we saw each other every day, as our jobs required us to work seven days a week. We might get a Sunday evening off during the off-season if the Brickman was empty for dinner. By Monday night, the hotel would once again be at full capacity. Technically, Jose didn't have to come to the kitchen for dinner, but since he didn't seem to have anything else to do, he was there most nights. He was helpful: If we needed someone to dish out vegetables as meals were being plated, he'd step in, or if we ran out of a meat dish, he would run downstairs to his butcher shop and race back up with a replacement.

But mostly, Jose wanted the company, enjoying the sense of friends and family, and having a place to be. Plus, he liked the wine. Many nights I would go into the lobby bar with two paper cups in hand and ask the bartender to fill them up. Jose and I would sit at the pink table and have a cup of wine together as the meal was being served. Once dinner was served, my only responsibility was to make sure things proceeded smoothly, which they usually did. So having a leisurely meal in a fast-paced environment over time, and over wine, became our routine. I enjoyed having Jose there.

Jose didn't seem to have much of a social life. I do not recall him speaking about dating or having a girlfriend. He spoke fluent English with the merest hint of an accent. I knew that he had come to the U.S. from a small town near Lima, Peru, but nothing about his life there. I knew nothing about his family or how he ended up as a kosher butcher in the Catskills. Jose had a great sense of humor and would make funny cracks about the staff, never in a cruel way. It was usually a take on someone's unique mannerisms. This would then prompt Jose to bestow a funny nickname on that person, which we would use as a shared secret code while the object of our attention raced around the kitchen.

We usually had lunch together with my dad and Chester, the chef. Dining with me was not easy. I liked eating off the plates of those I felt closest to, mostly Chester and Jose. They always seemed to have something that I didn't have but wanted. So I helped myself to the goodies on their plates. Jose's plate was always the most well-appointed. One time he made himself a salad that I instantly coveted: It was beautifully layered with sliced tomatoes, cucumbers and, my favorite, muenster cheese. Knowing that I couldn't resist invading his plate, he sprinkled cayenne pepper on the underside of the cheese. "Now, don't touch this, Patti, he said as he got up from the table. I'll be back in a half hour, and we can have lunch together."

"Okay," I said, and as soon as he left the kitchen. I grabbed a slice of cheese. Fire filled my mouth as a smiling Jose walked back in. He, my dad and Chester all started to laugh. One thing I did learn in the kitchen was how to curse, and the word "fuck" came spewing out of my mouth as the chef, Jose and my dad looked on in amusement.

Jose was a loyal employee, one of the few who didn't steal from us. Many employees thought loyalty meant it was within their right to steal from us. Guests too. We had to bolt down any TVs in the outlying buildings because, too often, guests would pull their car up to their accommodation and take the TV home with them. Each guest bathroom was equipped with lots of towels and washcloths, all white and plain, yet so many were stolen that we ended up stamping an ugly thick blue line down the center of them. Go figure; this increased the number of stolen towels. It got so bad with washcloths that we stopped providing them, offering them for sale in the smoke shop instead. One year we ordered coffee mugs with the name of the hotel printed on them. A nice touch for the dining room tables; we ordered thousands. Within weeks, they were all gone.

Some of our office staff stole from us, too. One employee was caught making off with reams of Brickman stationery. Why? I have no idea. Years before I was born, the chef at the time, Sam Maron, opened a restaurant in New York City and invited my dad, Murray and my grandparents to the opening. Our dishes, silverware and glassware were on each table, all "appropriated" from the Brickman. He was fired on the spot after having worked for my family for decades.

This brings me back to Chester. There was a limited supply of kosher chefs, and he was the best we ever had. I say this even though he liked to steal. Chester insisted Jose give him meat from our butcher shop to take home on the Sunday nights when we had off. He encouraged Jose to assist him in the thievery. After a few weeks of being strong-armed by Chester to make packages for him to take back to his family and friends, Jose told my dad what was happening. My dad had limited options; we needed Chester more than the meat. So my father told the chef he would have Jose make up a huge package of meat for him to take home whenever he had a Sunday night off. We now controlled how much he could, in effect, steal, which left Chester feeling happy and not quite so dishonest.

When you have few options, you go with what works, so at one point, when we learned that it was Jose supplying our staff with cocaine, we turned a blind eye. If we fired him, someone else would step in to do the dealing. As with kosher chefs, the supply of good kosher butchers was scarce; Jose was one of the best.

Chapter 24

Jewish Roots

South Fallsburg, New York

While the staff held a limitless fascination for me, our guests mostly seemed like a homogenous tide of New York City families. What we did share, what we knew was that our Judaism created a thread that wove us to one another. We each regarded and practiced our religion in our own particular way, but we identified as Jews. And in this corner of the Catskills, we knew we had the safety of the hotel and surrounding area to protect us from anti-Semitism in the wider world. There was a need for the Catskills — a place where we could live or vacation without the backdrop of hatred lurking in the shadows.

Most of the people that I knew from town were Jewish. A few were Christians (at the hotel, our kosher meals were being made by our Christian chef, baker, butcher and pantryman), but they joked that they were honorary Jews from living amongst us all. A few of the wait staff were older Jewish men. Almost everyone else was of color, especially during the 1970s and '80s, when many of the staff were from other countries.

I learned acceptance from the diverse environment of the hotel and from the secure enclave of my Jewish community. I learned who I am as a Jew and that if we look closely we have more in common with each other than with what separates us. I learned that the man who shared food with people in need knew more than the young woman working for her dad in the family business who never had to worry about her next meal. Scott Musgrave, a friend of mine and a member of the black community in town, told me that he did not feel the sting of racism until he went off to college and moved out of South Fallsburg. For the most part, the Catskills offered an accepting environment at home and work.

Yiddish was the language my dad heard at home as a young child and spoke it when talking to his parents (especially when he didn't want me to know what they were talking about, a typical application in Jewish homes). I wish I had learned to speak Yiddish. My father was interested in assimilating into American culture. I was more interested in preserving our Jewish culture. I know about 25 Yiddish words and like to use them with my Jewish friends, sometimes with Old World accents just for fun, which brings me back to the essence of who I am: a Jew.

The protective shield of my hometown community has ingrained itself into my core. I embrace the fact that Judaism is an anomaly. We are a culture, ethnicity and religion all at the same time. We have survived ghettos, pogroms and outright attempts to obliterate us. We have lived all over the globe as strangers in a strange land. How could I not love my hometown, an enclave where we could live in peace and not face the hatred and fear of much of the outside world? The irony is that if it weren't for the anti-Semitism, there would be no Catskills, where Jews found refuge.

As I search my memory, I keep returning to the diversity of our employees. As a child in the 1950s, I was especially fond of Zack and Helen Johnson, a gracious and dignified Caribbean couple who worked for us for many years, Helen cleaned guests' rooms, and Zack cleaned many of the top-tier staff rooms. One former coffee shop staffer remembers how he used to carefully remove the "roaches" before cleaning an ashtray, then putting the joint butts back in place when done.

There was A.D. Davis, who had the most contagious laugh. He worked for us for many years, mostly in maintenance. One year he was arrested for a minor offense and sentenced to jail. My dad stormed into the judge's office (this is part of small-town living) and "urged" the judge to allow A.D. to serve his sentence from Friday night to Sunday night. The judge obliged.

Matt Jones and his wife, Anna, were my neighbors, living across the street from me at the hotel. Matt, like A.D., was a year-round employee. One year, comedian Rodney Dangerfield was invited to live at the hotel for the summer. My uncle assumed Rodney would schmooze with the guests at the pool in the afternoons. Instead, Matt and Rodney became fast friends, and Rodney spent most of his time with Matt and Anna in their home.

We had several people on our wait staff from Brazil. Luis Petterson, which I knew was not his real name, was one of the most charismatic waiters we ever employed. He was so charming that even though I knew he had been arrested for selling cocaine, upon his release, he was back at work, serving our guests with a flair that was his alone. Luis was that good. He and his brother, Jose, were two of our best waiters. After a few years of loyal service, he asked if we would hire his niece and two nephews. On his word, we did, and within one season, all became part of our wait staff, where they remained until we sold the Brickman in 1986. Only years later did I learn that they were still teenagers when they came to work for us. And now, because of Facebook, I know that Luis' niece is a grandmother and one of his nephews is a dentist.

Many of the staff in the '70s and '80s were adult men and women, while some were teenagers who had fled the violence and poverty of their home countries in Central and South America. Most sent a large portion of their salaries and tips back home to help support their families. How often did a guest return a steak because it wasn't perfectly medium rare? Many of our staff had never even tasted a steak. What was important to our guests meant nothing to the young men working in our dining room.

Then there was Maria. She arrived in the U.S. from a small town near Bogotá, Columbia, about a year before she found her way to the Brickman. Within just a few months she became one of my favorite employees. Her hair was jet black, her skin tone cocoa, which offset the luster of her hair. Her eyes were so dark that her pupils melted into her irises, making you want to look deeper into them. Her uniform was always crisp and pressed; her white waitress shoes made her look older than her 24 years.

One morning I passed by her station while she was clearing dishes off a table. She looked up, took in my confident air, and said in her lively Spanish accent, "Your life is so charmed!" I smiled and thought my life *was* charmed. I lived at a resort hotel, I had a great job, a most adorable little daughter, the best father anyone could ask for, lots of good friends and a hometown I loved. Maria had looked at me as a role model of a successful young businesswoman, wife and mother. I seemed to have it all.

Her words swirled around me as the sun set in a pink and blue sky. As I approached my house, I noticed that the bedroom was dark. I stopped for a moment on the front porch. When I walked in, the quiet embraced me. Jo Anna was spending the night with my mother. I hoped I was alone. I crossed the living room and flicked on the light as I entered my bedroom. Sitting up on our bed, with two pillows positioned to support his heavy head, was Michael, nodding from his hallowed heroin. A reckoning was coming.

Chapter 25

The Pearl

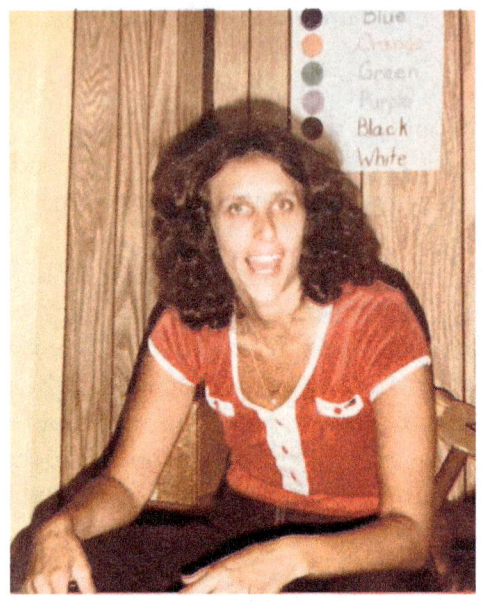

That's me in the late 1970s

"Come with me," my father said one clear fall day in 1984. There was a no-nonsense tone in his voice.

"Where are we going?" I was almost afraid to ask.

"To the apple orchard."

When I was a child, when the trees exposed their glorious colors and the apples were ripe for picking, my dad used to take me to the orchard. We'd fill our baskets with apples ready to be made into strudel, kugel and cider.

Now he opened the door to the car for me, and the expression on his face made me nervous. He looked fatherly and frightening at the same time. Sweet memories mixed with anxiety as we drove to the far end of the hotel property. He pulled over by the bridle path. Faint whiffs of manure entered the car. I wished I could gallop off on a horse.

"Patti," he began, "the chief of police called and told me he thinks Michael is selling and using drugs. Do you know about this?"

My mind wandered back to when I was a young girl, so happy to be picking apples with my dad. Peppy, our dog, often joined in, nibbling rotten apples that had fallen off the trees. Sometimes a porcupine would shed its quills into her nose, or a skunk would squirt its stink onto her, leaving her reeking until we got home to give her a bath of tomato juice.

I was shaking as I contemplated this question. "Dad, if that were true, wouldn't the police have arrested Michael?" I hoped my dad would absorb this as the truth.

He sighed and nodded in agreement. Shame drifted over me as we pulled back onto the road. We never spoke of this again. Neither of us wanted to accept the truth.

Several weeks later, I opened my bathroom door, stunned to find Michael stuffing paraphernalia for shooting up heroin into the breast pocket of his shirt.

"Are they yours?" I feared the answer and was sorry I asked. I hadn't thought about what I would have done if he had told me the truth. My denial was so powerful, I still needed it to protect me from the truth. I wasn't ready. Not yet.

Michael's quiet eyes spoke to me, *"You will believe what I am about to say"*

His verbal response, "I found them in the breakfast chef's room." I closed my eyes, took a breath and chose to believe this obvious lie.

Not long after, I wandered by the switchboard room and overheard the operator saying to a coworker, "She must pick up the phone and ask where Michael is at least ten times a day. Doesn't she know?" I stood there, feeling naked.

When the operator turned and saw me, her face turned white. I ran off, past the bellhop's desk, trying to find a place to hide. Doesn't *she know?* The words forced themselves past the barrier I had carefully built up over the past twenty years I had known Michael.

I didn't want to believe that my husband had a severe drug problem. But somewhere deep inside, I knew and had known all along. I suddenly realized that in addition to not knowing *where* he was most of the time, I didn't know *who* he was. The intelligent, charismatic, sexy young man I had befriended and then fell in love with was now a shell of what he had been. That split second of gossip punctured the first hole in my veil of denial.

Early mornings were the most difficult. Lying in bed next to Michael, I felt the dark web of hell clutch at me as I awoke. I often hurried into the shower, allowing hot water to cascade over me. I'd stand there yearning for a sense of cleanliness.

On other mornings, my young daughter nestled between us. On those days, I'd linger in bed, savoring the closeness of our child. Wrapping my arm around her, I felt a moment of stability. My routine, my child, my dad, my work and, most of all, my denial let me face the world with a mix of impending doom and many moments of joy.

Thanksgiving 1985 was the last time Michael lied to me about his whereabouts. And the last time I cared where he was. He had not come home the night before, and I was frantic all night. I had to find the strength to unravel myself from this insanity. Throughout the day, Jo Anna kept asking, "Where's daddy?" I had no answer. I stayed close to her, making up games and reading and singing to her.

The front door opened an hour before we were to leave to meet my parents at a lovely inn for our holiday dinner. I heard Michael go to the closet before he entered the living room. He stood there momentarily as Jo Anna ran over and hugged his legs. He reached down and patted her head. We asked in unison, "Where have you been?" Michael remained silent. I sat still, watching the last rays of the sun set behind the field at the back of our home. Finally, he spoke.

"Just give me a few minutes to shower and change, and we can meet your parents for dinner." He said this as if he hadn't been missing for almost 24 hours. I nodded as I took Jo Anna's hand.

I didn't ask him where he had been until we came home from dinner and Jo Anna was asleep. In a soft voice, he told me he had been with Carole, his girlfriend. I wished he had shoved a knife into my heart instead of telling me the truth. I had trouble finding my breath. The following day, I told him to leave.

Michael was the one who took Jo Anna to Wendy's to tell her that we would be getting a divorce. I was sitting on the couch when they came home, immobile from fear and anticipation. Jo Anna, tears in her eyes, looked up at her dad, knowing she would soon have to say goodbye. She came into my lap and hugged me, pressing heavily on my breasts. Michael sat next to us and kissed her on the forehead. Then he looked at me and said, "I'll go pack some stuff."

I was frightened that first night after Michael left. I was alone. In my home. With my child. I pictured my younger self in his Bronx apartment just before we married, when Michael saturated himself full of heroin. My older self nodded to her as she began to fade away.

Later that night, silence surrounded me, fraying the edges of the veil that obscured the reality of my life with Michael. The January wind whipped around my home, and the icicles fused to the eaves. The full moon gleamed over fields of snow, its beams peeking through the lace curtains that framed my living room windows. Jo Anna was tucked into her bed.

Into the silence, I screamed. The sound hammered through the quiet of my house, resonating around the contours of each room, then recoiled back. I shut my eyes and screamed again as I pulled at my hair. I felt I might go insane. Darkness knew me well. I don't know if Jo Anna heard me. As the last vibration rolled off my tongue, a gentle wind pushed me just close enough to the edge of the precipice to savor insanity. Closing my eyes, I screamed one last time. I felt a slight draft. Then an unfamiliar breeze swept across the room. I sat still as a chill caressed my skin. When I finally opened my eyes, I glanced toward the foyer and imagined my veil of denial limping out the door. The veils I had created were intricate, handmade, exquisite and expensive.

Denial is like looking through a stained glass window. I could see through the window, but the colors distorted my view. Denial seduced me, keeping me alive and sane until I could find the courage to listen to what was hiding within me. And then, I heard a voice within me say, *"You have a choice. You can be the best that you can be, or you can be the best that you can be."*

You can be the best you can be. And there I was left with the question: How do I do this? What does this mean? Denial had tugged at me for many years as I tried to create a story to fit the narrative of what I perceived my life should be. Denial had kept me alive and sane until I could find the courage to explore my life. Listening in the right moment allowed harmony to resonate. I had no choice but to pay attention.

I had to move forward to save myself and my child. It was a slow process. *Be the best you can be;* my hidden voice was sending a message I have come to cherish. I've given that voice a name — Grace. I will never forget the quiet permeating the room that night as Grace spoke in hushed tones. I succumbed to the calm that embraced me. She has been a gentle and powerful chaperone since that dark night. Her voice is subtly different from the texture of mine. She shows up in the corners of my dreams, on the pages of my journal.

As the sun rose, the light began to peek through the windows. I turned off the lamp in the living room, allowing the natural light to shape the day.

Each scream had further parted the veils that had shielded me from the truth that Michael was a heroin addict, a junkie. And I was complicit; I kept him going. His brilliance, character and charisma evaporated bit by bit every time he put a needle in his vein. He was now a shell. I was the pearl.

Chapter 26

Uncle Murray Checks Out

Violetta Loarca, my dad and Uncle Murray, toward the end

August 1985. "Good Morning, Patti," Uncle Murray said in a tender voice that brought me back to the magic tricks he used to buy for me on his trips to New York City when I was a kid. I immediately knew something was wrong. He hadn't spoken to me in that tone since I was a child. I felt a bit uneasy.

A few minutes later, I went into the dining room to see Karl Tagman, our maitre d'. Karl was a wonderful man, always with a smile, as if nothing terrible had ever happened to him. During World War II, when he was a teenager in Hungary, he had been separated from his parents, sister and twin brother, never knowing what had happened to them.

When Karl was in his mid-50s, he found his way to the Brickman. One of the things he loved to do after work was to go to the racetrack in Monticello. Like many of the waiters and busboys who worked for him, he could be found there several nights a week. On Tuesday nights, we hired a bus to take the many guests who wanted a night at the track.

One night while at the racetrack, a stranger walked up to Karl and said, "Mr. Tagman, I know your brother and sister. They are living in Israel." I can only imagine how this news must have struck Karl. This stranger, who was friends with Karl's siblings, had somehow figured out that our Karl Tagman was originally Karol Tajgman in his native Hungary. For 35 years, Karl thought his family had been slaughtered in Europe. And now he knew that, while his parents had indeed perished, his siblings had survived. As it turned out, they thought that their brother Karol had died. They all had a joyous reunion that winter in Israel.

As I walked into the dining room, I saw the worried look on Karl's face. He told me something strange had happened when Murray entered the dining room. Murray couldn't remember the name of his waiter. Odd, I thought.

It turned out that odd didn't come close to what was happening to my uncle. My dad kept an eye on him all day. Murray seemed off, but it was subtle. A verbal stumble, a name or number said incorrectly, was all we noticed. Around 3 p.m., my dad and uncle went to the coffee shop for ice cream. There, Murray's long- and short-term memory completely disappeared, as if in an instant. He suddenly morphed into a docile and demented 74-year-old man. From then on, he only knew his immediate family. And Sandy. He forgot how to feed himself or that he needed to eat. He forgot how to take care of his most basic needs. His stern eyes were now a haze. The solitude of his heart was exposed in a slight smile.

My dad and Helen moved Uncle Murray into the apartment that had been his parents, which was right above his home. They provided round-the-clock caretakers to feed, dress, wash and care for his every need. One day at the beginning of this journey, he somehow got out of his apartment in his underwear and disappeared. Our staff was commandeered to search for him. They found him, wandering and frightened, near the staff quarters on the way to the day camp. After that, he was never left alone.

Helen, for the first time in their marriage, stood up to one of his mistresses. It was the first time she could. She forbade Sandy from visiting Murray. Simple as that. But Sandy snuck in to see him whenever she could. My father visited him every day. I visited often. He was no longer my adversary. He was soft-spoken, sad and loving.

Sometimes my dad would bring him into the reservation office. He often looked perplexed. I remember walking past him one day and saying, "Hi, Uncle Murray." Two minutes later, I walked past him again. And he said with a Yiddish inflection, "You don't say hello?" His memory was lost, but his comedic tendencies remained.

That August was the first time in my dad's life that he didn't have his older brother as his partner. The relationship between "the boys" had been at an all-time low, thanks to Sandy. The first change my dad made was to tell Sandy to sit on the sidelines for the remainder of the season and not come back the following year. It made such a difference. Suddenly this negative force was neutralized; it would soon disappear completely.

My father delegated more responsibilities to me, and we all pulled together to manage the hotel. Although things ran smoothly, business was off, as it had been for the past few years — for us, as well as most of the other hotels in the Catskills.

At that point my dad was 72, I was 35 and recently separated from Michael. I was worried about what would happen to my dad, me and the hotel if Murray, 74, were to die. This now was a real possibility.

In wondering about the future of the Brickman, I thought back to my last major fight with Murray just weeks before his memory vanished. I wish I remembered what triggered that argument. We were in the reservation office. Our discussion got heated. Drawing the attention of the office staff, we both knew to retreat to his private office. He took his seat at his desk as if we were following a script. I walked around to the other side of his desk, my position for our discussions. He motioned for me to sit. I refused. I never sat during our confrontations.

At one point, he glared at me and said, "I don't care what happens to the hotel if I die." With that, I asked if he had a will. "I do not," he said, just a little too loud.

"But if something ever happens to your dad," he continued, "then I will own the hotel, one hundred percent." Startled, I took a breath. Thinking of my dad's death was unbearable, I couldn't imagine my life without him. I had to compose myself. I had to think this through. If something were to happen to my father, my mother would inherit his shares of the hotel, and as their only child, I was the "heir apparent." Murray and Helen never had children, and their sister never had any shares in the hotel.

My mother simply could not take on the responsibilities of running anything, let alone a hotel. I would have to step up to do this. I looked down at Murray, put my hand out as if to shake his and said, "If something happens to my dad, say hello to your new partner." With that, I turned around and walked out, slamming the door to his office as I left.

I knew I had to completely understand all the possibilities that could transpire when one of "the Posner boys" died. I knew that one day I would inherit my dad's half of the hotel. It was uncertain who would inherit Murray's shares. Both men were in their 70s. Murray had this bizarre memory loss (attributed to Alzheimer's and other related dementias). I played out the scenarios I could imagine. My future and finances were in play and in jeopardy. I had to understand this.

The following day, at the pink table, I asked my beloved dad if he had a will. I was stunned when he said no. "Well, you need to get one," I told him. I then recounted my latest confrontation with his brother and explained the different scenarios if Murray and/or Helen died. There were no good options. Finally, I told him, "You can leave me broke. You can leave me with money, but please do not leave me in debt. Or with partners I can't work with." He smiled sheepishly and hugged me.

"Okay, okay," he said. "Let's find a lawyer."

That felt good. Not only did my dad hear me, but he agreed with me. I still wonder where I found the strength to say these words to him. Or how, at the age of 35, I figured out the various scenarios of who could potentially own shares of the hotel. Only weeks later, at what turned out to be our last angry encounter, charismatic Murray was a shell of his former self.

The new lawyer turned out to be an old friend of the hotel. My dad had asked the Stricklers if they could recommend someone, and they recommended Stanley Rogovin. Stan had come to work for us when he was just 17 and now was one of the best estate attorneys in New York City. Even with my dad's will and trust being compiled, there was no good scenario for us as to who would inherit Murray's shares of the Brickman. The line of succession for our family hotel was now an urgent matter.

Our overall future was precarious. The Catskill resort industry had been declining for years as more Jews assimilated into American culture, as women became more prevalent in the workforce, as air conditioning made summer in the city more tolerable. In addition, air travel increasingly made the world more accessible, and the need to spend time in the Catskills was waning.

On a warm October day in 1986, I was standing under the breezeway of the main building with my dad. The leaves had already turned from their vibrant colors to muted hues. We were chatting, as usual, about the fate of the hotel. I knew that if Murray died, my dad would be in a pickle, and as that pickle fermented, I'd be screwed.

These were trying times. Rumors of the sale of the Brickman had started to run rampant that spring. Soon after Murray lost his memory, they escalated. One persistent story was that the SYDA Foundation, the ashram just down the road from the hotel, was interested in buying it. But these were just rumors. We had not considered selling our family business. And then . . .

As we were standing under the breezeway, I noticed a man walking up the driveway. I turned back to my dad, and we continued examining our options if Murray died. The man waved to us, trying to get our attention. He seemed to know who my dad was. He had a welcoming smile.

"I hear we are buying the Brickman," he said as if this were an everyday statement. My dad turned to me. I thought to give himself a moment to find a punchline to a joke.

"How much are we paying?" my dad asked. "Give me a number," the man replied.

My dad thought for a few minutes. There was a puzzled look on his face, but a softness appeared just before he turned to face this stranger. My dad told the man the amount of money he thought the hotel was worth. As if this conversation had been rehearsed, the man said, "We have a deal." He reached out and shook my dad's hand.

The man, it turned out, was the buying agent for the SYDA Foundation. And just like that, so suddenly, so surprisingly — we sold the Brickman. We closed the deal six weeks later, on December 17, 1986. The hotel had been in our family for 74 years.

The sale is official

We now knew how the final chapter of the Hotel Brickman would play out. Selling it to the SYDA Foundation was the best solution to what I perceived as an unsolvable problem. My dad knew that the hotel revenues were declining, and now he would be guaranteed financial stability. The decline of our business was inevitable. Most of the other major resorts in the area were failing. Many had already gone bankrupt. Had we not taken this offer, I would have another story to tell.

As soon as the papers were signed, I looked up at my dad, wondering how he felt. He was selling more than a business; he was selling a piece of Jewish history, a family legacy, a way of life. He was selling all he had ever been, all he had ever known. He was also selling the hotel to an organization that would claim an educational tax exemption which meant our tiny town of South Fallsburg, now in financial decline, would have a major property taken off the tax rolls.

He also would have to tell our employees that they would be losing their livelihoods. This lay heavily on my dad. We discussed this often in the two months between the offer and the closing. Several people were year-round employees, and five families lived on the hotel grounds, including my Aunt Helen and me. We would all have to find new homes, new lives. I asked him how we would move on. He said simply, "We will make new traditions." And so we did.

The sale laid heavy on my dad, though. In a letter he wrote to his sister soon after the sale, he shared with her, *"It will take another month before all the affairs of the hotel will be wind down, and then there will be no more Brickman. It's heartbreaking. I cried like a baby upon the closing, but there was no other choice for me."*

On May 10, 1912, Abraham Brickman founded the Hotel Brickman. The almost 97 acres he purchased included "a 60-room boardinghouse, 1 kerosene stove, 1 butter churn, 1 dinner bell, 1 two-seat top wagon, and 2 pigs." Two pigs, the only animals on what was to become one of the premier kosher resorts in the Catskills. When the hotel was sold, we had 207 acres that had been home to 70 buildings housing 300 guest rooms, multitudes of staff rooms, a day camp, a basketball court, a baseball field, nine tennis courts, three pools, a nightclub and what had been my home for 36 years.

On December 23, 1987, a year after we sold the hotel, my Uncle Murray passed away quietly at age 75. A heavy smoker for years, often going through five packs of cigarettes a day, he died of cardiac arrest.

What I have come to know over all these years since the hotel was sold is that I am blessed it was part of my life, but not for all of my life. The sale set me free to create a new life, to create new experiences, to find new love, to go from being Patti-from-the-Brickman to being the artist of my own life.

Chapter 27

Country Roads

My husband, Yossi Daboosh, painted these
during our month in the country.

In the fall of 2004, the opportunity presented itself to rent a small apartment on Lake Louise Marie, just a few miles from South Fallsburg. My third, best and final husband, Yossi Daboosh, and I rented it sight unseen. Running through my head was the question, can I go home again? We'd be in the Catskills for the month of October. I hadn't spent that much time there since we sold the hotel. A year after we sold it, Jo Anna and I moved to Fort Lee, New Jersey.

My dad had a home in South Florida but still had his home in South Fallsburg and spent every summer up there. He was the main reason I wanted to spend time in my hometown. The county's natural beauty was perfect for my artist husband to paint.

Our daily routine was settled early on. Having coffee on the dock near our apartment, the expanse of nature before us, became our morning ritual, setting the tone for our entire visit. I hadn't expected that. I had thought that running into old friends would be the highlight of my return to South Fallsburg or that remembering all the characters who had worked at the hotel would fill my thoughts. But the stillness and the quiet of the lake brought me home. In the early morning, mist streamed off the lake, rising like a ghost, clouding our view of the trees and making them pale green. Then it evaporated before our eyes. After coffee, Yossi and I walked along roads that eased around the lake and skirted the forest.

Something was ephemeral about the sun's rays glistening off a metal boat shed, the half-obscured houses tucked into the evergreens and the trees changing color with each passing day, noting autumn's progress. The lake was dark, the color of coffee with just a touch of milk, with hardly a ripple to disturb its glossy surface. It was the stillness I came to love.

From late morning to mid-afternoon, Yossi painted, and I wrote. One of his favorite spots was in nearby Bethel, the site of the iconic Woodstock concert. Yossi arranged his reds, blues and yellows to capture the barns, sky, dirt paths and trees while I set up my computer, hoping to capture the mood of my hometown experience. Occasionally there would be a sound, a squirrel, the chirp of a bird or the crunch of leaves. And then, for a moment, silence. All this brought me back to my years living in South Fallsburg, where natural beauty surrounded me. I had taken all this for granted then, and now I cherished it.

I was beginning to feel at home. After all, I still was a "local," having been born in the Catskills. I looked forward to recreating the life I lived to see if I could go home again. What would it offer me, if anything?

When I first stepped into my dad's home, the home I grew up in, I wondered what it would be like to stay here again. Would I be lulled to sleep by the furnace, as I had been my whole childhood? As I walked up the hallway, I heard it creak, reminding me of my mother making her way to her bedroom, holding her cup of Sanka, leaving the droplets on the floor.

It was almost impossible to go into my parents' bedroom. It looked the same; I waited for my mother to reappear. A year before she passed, my father finally revealed to her that he had told me she had lied about her age. But my mother and I never talked about it. The night before she died, she took her engagement ring off her finger and handed it to me. I slipped it on my finger tenderly. It was a moment of intimacy that I had longed for. On September 16, 1993, my mother died at home. She was 84. And she was 78.

After leaving their bedroom, I found my dad in the den, with its dark paneled walls and large picture window that looked out onto the expansive backyard. I sat in the chair next to him, as I had done so many times before. When I looked up, I knew he would be smiling with the smile he saved just for me. At the hotel and at his home, my dad often sat with me at his desk, his hands clenched behind his head, elbows splayed.

He was my father, my friend, my mentor and my boss. I knew at a very young age that I had a choice, to see the world through the clear lens he looked through, or through the cracked lens of my mother. It was an easy choice to make. He taught me to be an optimist, to accept change readily and to accept all kinds of people lovingly, to have a bit of whimsy and never to eat celery. Bacon, yes, Celery, no.

After we left my dad's that afternoon, I asked Yossi to drive through South Fallsburg. A chill ran through me as we drove down Main Street. The town looked like an old man who had lost too many teeth and could not afford a dentist. The street was studded with abandoned buildings with cracked panes of glass, the sidewalks broken. The restaurants and shops I loved to visit were all gone, and Hasidim, ultra-Orthodox Jews, ran the stores that replaced most of them, now dominating the area. All this wrinkled my memories.

Just as I was despairing of finding anything or anyone of comforting familiarity, a voice rang out: "Patti Posner?" That's what I was waiting for. My old friend, Ira Gold, peered in a little closer before repeating my name. "Patti," this time as a statement, not a question. As I turned around, I felt like a local again. Then he gave me that smile, the one I had known since kindergarten, a smile so grand that I wanted to move back home just so I could once again be a part of this community that I was not sure still existed.

The happiness that surrounded me after my conversation with Ira lasted the rest of the day. When I lived there, it would take a long time to walk the few blocks that comprised South Fallsburg, having to stop often to chat, but on that day, there was only Ira to say hello to.

After our stroll through town, Yossi and I took a drive on the country roads that were so familiar to me. I opened my window to feel the breeze. I heard the chirp of crickets, a sound I so often fell asleep to in our little summer cottage behind the Ranch House at the Brickman. It felt like my childhood was hugging me. It was so good to fill my eyes, ears and heart with these tangible memories. The sights and sounds of the country were taking me home.

While we were taking in the views of my Catskills, I told Yossi that I wanted to drive out to the Glen Wild Cemetery. I explained to him that it's more than just a place to bury our dead. It's a place that holds the memories of the past generations who made the Catskills a safe haven when we needed a place to call our own. It recalls a time when my grandparents were the community's elders. If I had remained there, I would now be holding that torch.

The back roads took us to the hamlet of Glen Wild, a rural community moments away from becoming a ghost town. The ride there was glorious. In spring and summer, ferns weaved through the surrounding forest floor; in fall, the leaves spread out like a quilt. Near collapse, an old barn peered over the hill's crest. Past the barn was a farmhouse, with a 1947 Chevy truck rusting silently beside it, a sign that the cemetery was approaching. As we got closer, I could feel the history of my people embracing me, a feeling I've had each time I've returned there.

We strolled among the gravestones. I wanted Yossi to "know" the people of my hometown. We stopped at the grave of Sam Beytin. "His daughter, Joyce, has been my friend since kindergarten," I told him. "Sam, Mr. Beytin, was my science teacher in high school and the maitre d' at the hotel when I was a kid."

Over at the largest plot in the cemetery, we sat on a bench, and I introduced Yossi to Rose and Louis Perlstein. "They were my grandparents' best friends. He built my dad's house in 1948. Their daughter, Gert, and her husband were my parents' good friends." I point to her grave and continue. "When I was a kid, my parents had parties at our house. Gert and her husband were always there. I hated those parties. Everyone was drinking and, I suppose, having fun. But I didn't realize it then. I felt trapped in my room when they were all there." I surprised myself with the passion in my voice. My eyes were moist. "If I got too upset, my mom came into my room. Her breath smelled of alcohol. She'd lean in, closer than she normally did. Sometimes I felt a moment of tenderness from her."

After visiting the Perlsteins, I introduced Yossi to our town's shopkeepers and businessmen, their wives and children, and many other friends of my family.

Finally, it was time to show Yossi where my family was buried. The sun began to descend into billows of white clouds, and shadows danced around the graves. There, under a large oak tree, was my family's plot, an enormous headstone welcoming us with the name POSNER.

"Meet my grandparents," I said as if we were standing before them. "And this must be Uncle Murray," Yossi said as if he were meeting him in person. "Thanks to the many stories you've told me, I feel like I know him!" I walked over to my mother's grave. Bending down to get closer to it, I pulled some weeds out of the ground. Within minutes after we left the solemnity of the cemetery, I was enjoying the sight of cows eating out of a trough near a peeling red barn. I loved the rich odor of manure; it reminded me of the horse stable we had at the hotel.

Four years later, on July 3, 2008, I would visit the cemetery again. This time I knelt by my father's grave. Tears filled my eyes. For my whole life, my dad was the one I went to for almost everything. He was the one who got me up in the morning for school, who made me breakfast and took me out for dinners. As a teenager, he bought most of my clothes, chauffeured me around and helped me with homework. As an adult, he entrusted me with running the hotel kitchen and supported me through two divorces. As he was dying, he entrusted his life to me, asking me to make all of his medical decisions.

My dad died in our home in Boca Raton, Florida, on June 29, 2008, at the age of 93. I was at his side. Years before, when we interred my mom, there was a huge rock where her coffin was to be placed, so she was buried in the space reserved for my dad. A few weeks before my dad died, I called Steve Altman, president of the local synagogue and a family friend, to discuss what we would do if that rock could not be removed. Steve and I emailed back and forth about this somber task, which we called Reservations for Ben Posner in keeping with a hotel theme.

When my dad passed, Steve sent in a backhoe to remove the rock. Only it wasn't a large rock — it was the tiny casket of my parents' first-born daughter. Paula's casket was repositioned so we could bury my dad next to my mom. As they lowered him into his grave, I sat by Paula's small headstone, sharing this moment in the passing of our father.

Before leaving the cemetery, I walked over to my mother's grave and placed a stone on her grave. Then, I placed a stone on Paula's grave.

Epilogue

My dad and me

The leaves were losing their early-autumn brilliance, their colors becoming muted, the shade of rusted trucks. Clouds hung from the sky, reminding me of my grandmother's white hair tinged with blue. It was all so familiar, the hills and valleys covered with evergreen, birch and maple trees, lush in the summer, now preparing for their winter sleep.

Time flies and slows down simultaneously. Or so it seemed as we wound down our time in the mountains. The days grew chilly, the nights almost cold. It rained often, and the lake looked gloomy. The leaves peaked and now lay on the ground, waiting to be covered by winter's snow. And yet I didn't want to leave.

* * *

After our month in the mountains, I gathered up my memories and planted them in my new homes. First, in my life in South Florida, and now in Weaverville, North Carolina, where I once again drive on country roads and look at mountains every day — not the Catskills, but the Blue Ridge.

I thought the hotel would vanish from my life when we sold it. But the passage of time brings rich new meanings to my memories. Growing up in a resort hotel is an all-inclusive experience. For almost four decades, the Brickman was my home, my life and my work. The lobby was my living room, hospitality was the foundation of my life experiences. It taught me leadership as well as teamwork, flexibility, crisis management, multitasking and respect, skills that helped me navigate the world when I no longer was Patti-from-the-Brickman. But what had the most profound effect on me was having the world come to me. I had the privilege of living and working with men and women from diverse backgrounds, cultures and experiences, which taught me acceptance, kindness and love.

My story is more than one of growing up in a Catskills resort hotel owned for generations by my family. It's a story of denial and pain, fun and friends, and a litany of unforgettable characters. It's also a story of Jewish tradition, hopes and fears, all seeping into me through the people, the culture, the food and the history of the Catskill Mountains.

The Catskills are never far from my mind, and if I mention that I grew up there, I often hear a delighted cry of recognition. Even at a book club in Weaverville, N.C., a new member asked if I was from New York. She recognized my New York accent, even though I have incorporated "y'all" into my vocabulary. When I told her I grew up at the Hotel Brickman, her face lit up as if she had just met a rock star. "My family went there for years!" she enthused. "My best memories are from those summers!"

And for the umpteenth time, I got to tell someone how blessed I am that the place I still call home brings them such joyous recollections. It fills me up.

The Brickman brings me smiles, memories, strength and a unique way to see the world. It has been 36 years since we sold the hotel, but the passage of time makes it clearer that I am who I am because of my view from the mountains.

OTHER VOICES

BEN POSNER
(From notes written in the early 1990s)

When I was a kid in South Fallsburg, my school was at the bottom of the hill, just past the hotel. I remember sliding to school on a sled. Our next-door neighbor, Ben Selbst, would come by on his Flexible Flyer, and Murray would jump on him, and I would jump on Murray, and the three of us slid right up to the entrance of the school. It was a one-room schoolhouse with a woodshed and two outhouses, built in 1845 and closed about 1930.

During the late 1920s, we were open all winter and had about 30 guests. Most were sick or recovering and stayed one or two months. In the morning, I would set the table and help my mother and grandmother get ready for breakfast, then I would leave for school. After school, I would help serve and clean up dinner. We had just one employee, Emil Kobus, who had come from Poland. He milked our 11 cows — we used to sell the milk to some of our neighbors — and he took care of our four horses, several pigs and our many chickens. My mother was the cook and chambermaid, my father was the chauffeur, farmer and general handyman, and my grandmother took care of the records and also helped with the cooking.

In winter, we heated the hotel with wood-burning and coal stoves. After school, I would go with Emil into the woods to cut down trees, trim off the branches and, with a horse, drag the logs out to a clearing near the barn. Then we would cut the logs up into 16-inch lengths, and then Emil would cut them into smaller pieces for the cooking stove or the big boiler in the basement.

I think 1929 was the last year we were open all year. We could only accommodate those 30 people in the winter house. All the rest were summer rooms. After the stock market crash, business fell off, and it didn't pay for us to stay open.

MURRAY POSNER
(From an interview conducted in December 1978)

Murray and Ben

I was a skinny kid, and when we were out in the barn, my father would take an egg out of the nest, poke holes on the top and bottom and make me drink it to give me strength. My mother loved to tell about how when we didn't have enough eggs from our chickens, she would buy them from the store — but our boarders didn't want them from a store.

They thought that fresh eggs were health-giving. So she would take the eggs out to the barn, dirty them with chicken manure, put them in a basket and put some feathers in there. That made the guests happy.

The Depression had a very strong effect on our business. I have a book showing the house count from 1932 on, and I got pages in July with 40 people in the hotel, 60 people. Rates were $22.50 a week, $25 a week. The Elm Shade was down to $18.50, $20 a week, and everybody was cutting everybody else to try to do some business. In some other places, waiters and busboys worked just for tips, and they were happy to get the jobs. We used to pay them $10 a week. In June, we'd get musicians to work for nothing, for room and board, and during the summer, they might get $15-$20 a week. Everybody would cut help because they didn't have the money to pay them.

After World War II, there was a period of expansion up here, and it has never stopped, so our hotel is really a construction business, a restaurant business, a nightclub business. We run a children's camp, an athletic center. You've got to be an engineer and an interior decorator. These are all the things that we're doing all the time. But we're still farmers, and we're still taking care of the grounds and planting shrubs and trees.

BART CHARLOW

My Fallsburg friend, whose family owned the Irvington Hotel

We lived two lives. One riotous short span of the Catskill resort season, the other nine months of sublime country living. I loved them both, though much of the winter was spent longing for the blessed summer.

Paintbox fall with her gorgeous warm to crisp days. Butterflies and wildflowers followed by woodsmoke and the crinkle of the leaves beneath our feet in the woods or on the streets. School and small-town life, familiar, accessible, steady and seeming to be there forever.

Dark winters cocooning from the snow. Light sparkling from the ice crystals that made the bare trees into chandeliers on mornings of low-rising suns. Sledding on snow days to the music of tire chains on the roads.

Short and hopeful springs, when streams ran icy even as the snow melted and the land warmed to its future. Waiting weekends for city folks to tentatively nose back into reopening hotels and bungalows, testing the "merchandise" before buying their vacation breaks. Greening woods under warm showers, and the flies and the guests would return in swarms.

Then the magical season of summer! Oiled bodies cooking in the sun by the pool. Kids splashing and flashing their joy at camp.

Romance by the week and weekend, love won, lost and forgotten. Massive menus, all you could and did eat. Comics and *tummlers* and rhumba bands. Groups of teens playing baseball and eyeing one another through puberty. Parents inadvertently teaching us about the vagaries of human behavior, their loves and infidelities, their egos and insecurities played out against a cast of waiters, bellhops and bungalow bunnies. Colored spotlights illuminating the fantasy of hotel architecture and hotel life, and hotel promise on endlessly long evenings.

And for 10 weeks, we were kings and queens of our known universe. I tell folks we were "carnies," carnival people, but we never moved the tents. We hotel brats went from ho-hum bumpkins to little princes and princesses and later to hard workers toiling at whatever needed an extra hand. We knew everything and everyone and even more than we could ever imagine until age taught us what we'd had all along and what we should have known.

Our family's Hotel Irvington, born of a farm in a poor farming country, led to such a rich life. Our hotel families were intertwined, sometimes competitors, other times collaborators. And then in the end, the dying embers of a way of life that will never be replicated again.

I envy you, Patti, my sister, my friend. You lived it through to the finish, while I abandoned it for the world too early, or maybe just in time.

LARRY STRICKLER
Brickman activities director, 1965–1986

When I was 17, in 1958, I got the opportunity to work at a small Catskills resort, singing and emceeing. From there I worked at several hotels, including the Loch Sheldrake Inn, the Grand Mountain and Gilbert's. I found my way to the Brickman at age 24 and spent 21 summers and many weekends and holiday periods there, remaining until it closed in 1986. I spent the last 25 years of my 50-year-plus Catskills career at another great hotel, Kutsher's Country Club.

The Brickman is special because when I got there, I knew I had made it. The Concord and Grossinger's were a tad more famous, but the Brickman was among the gold-standard hotels, noted for its food, entertainment, day camp, teen program, tennis courts, Olympic pool and more. And my job was to create a fun-filled experience for thousands of guests as the activities director. I like to say my job was to manufacture fun. I was getting room and board for my family and me, plus a salary doing what I loved to do — entertaining, singing, making people happy, and doing all of this with two great bosses.

Ben and Murray treated me with love and respect. Two brothers. Two very different personalities. Ben, the warm behind-the-scenes guy who, quietly and without fanfare, kept the hotel humming. Murray was the consummate charming front man with a nose for talent. They ran a tight ship and, along with their wives, made me, my wife Shelly and my children, Karyn, Marcy and Sari, feel like family.

Ben's daughter Patti was and remains family. We forged a relationship even when she was a teen. We remained close friends through her jobs as a hotel operator and kitchen steward, through her marriage(s), and right up to today. I relish the sheer joy and memories of working at this wonderful resort and being part of its history.

SHELLY STRICKLER

Summers at the Brickman shaped me in so many ways during the prime of my life, from 24 to 45 years old, from 1965 to 1986. It was with me from young motherhood and teaching, through my children's teen years and a career in broadcast journalism. It taught me about life, friendship, love and perseverance.

I had known the "mountains" all my life. My parents took my sister and me to bungalow colonies and small hotels every summer. When I married Larry, he had already begun his journey working at various smaller hotels until he landed at Brickman's in 1965.

For me, the hotel was great in so many ways. Spending summers there during my Brooklyn teaching years with my twin girls and later a third girl was to enjoy a haven away from cooking, cleaning, even child care. My children were well taken care of at the day camp. It also introduced me to leisure activities I would never have experienced in Brooklyn. I learned how to play tennis and lounged on the pool decks; I experienced the incredible shows for which the Catskills were so famous. I loved the three sumptuous meals a day, followed in the evening, after showtime, by a fourth meal in the coffee shop (maybe I should have skipped that one). I relished the Jewish holiday rituals held at the hotel, complete with famous cantors and choirs.

When I became a radio journalist in 1978, Brickman's became where I would escape on my two days off and two-week vacations. It was an immersion into the head-clearing fresh air, walks in the country, swimming, good food, tennis and so much more. But perhaps the most satisfying and enduring part of my Brickman experience was the friendships I made. Patti Posner Daboosh remains among our very closest friends to this day, which is remarkable in that I arrived at the hotel at the age of 24 while Patti was just 14.

Mel Simons, the other emcee, also remains a dear friend to this day and is still the incorrigible character he was at the hotel. Rochelle Kovar, the dining room hostess who recently passed away, completed our inseparable foursome.

Oh, the fun we had. Many words have been written about the heyday of the Catskills. Some mourn its passing. I don't. I lived it. I loved it. And my memories are always with me.

Patti Posner

MARCY STRICKLER
Karyn's twin sister

In May of 1982, I had just finished my freshman year at George Washington University and was deciding whether or not I should do something different that summer. Since 1965, I had spent every summer at the Brickman. It was hard to imagine doing anything else. My sister Karyn was dating a guy in Brooklyn and decided to work at a diner in Sheepshead Bay while taking a math course at Brooklyn College. But even her toe-step into independence didn't sway me to strike out on my own, so back to Brickman's, I went.

Although not the children of a hotel owner, my sisters and I certainly acted like we ran the place. Every Sunday, we parked ourselves in the main lobby and introduced ourselves to the teenagers who appeared to be our age. Some of them recognized us from previous summers. We were the mainstays. Twins, no less. Two identical faces, easy for them to recognize. In fact, Brickman was one of the few places where we were regularly referred to as "The Twins," called such by the bellhops, waiters, busboys, lifeguards and counselors.

At the time, it was hard to fully appreciate how unique and special the experience was. Looking back, I lived the life of a princess in a castle, free to roam the grounds and take full advantage of its amenities. If I wanted to go horseback riding, I'd just head to the stables. If I wanted to play tennis, I'd go to the courts. If I wanted to swim laps, I'd be in the indoor pool. If I wanted to dance at night, there was the disco. If I wanted to laugh, I'd go see a comedian in the nightclub. I'd have whatever my heart desired for breakfast, a full-course meal every night and a game room full of pinball machines.

I'm glad I returned to the hotel that year, even without Karyn. I knew it would probably be my last summer in the Catskills, and it was.

KARYN STRICKLER
Marcy's twin sister

Marcy and Karyn

Growing up as a teenager in the late 1970s, I experienced some formative years at the Brickman as one of the "hotel brats," as kids of staff members were lovingly called. My experience is more of a "we" than a "me" since most stories center around my twin sister, Marcy, and myself. Unlike guests, who were generally there only for a week at a time, we were mainstays and would meet new friends every Sunday, then part with them by week's end with the anticipation of making a brand new set of friends to be in charge of. I say "in charge of" because we dictated how their vacation time went for them!

Looking back, it was somewhat egomaniacal and a feeling of superiority that led us to that role. If we participated in activities, then they participated with us. If we rebelled to do our own thing, we had instant followers to be "bad" with. Without a doubt, my most fun years were 1976 to 1980 — the "Disco Years." At ages 13 and 14, it was more innocent fun, but we were around older staff members and were impressionable. I "experimented" with pot at 13, experienced my first kiss at 14, my first love at 16, not to mention my first heartbreak and even my first "Me Too" moment.

The atmosphere was one of great freedom: Sneaking out at night to hang out in the lobby felt dangerous, but in hindsight, we did nothing crazy. Just hang out and talk and smoke a little weed. From age 15 to 18, our days mostly involved lounging around the pool, but nights were spent at neighboring hotels and discos. Monday night was the Raleigh's Mambo Night; Thursday night was spent at the Stag and Doe Disco in Monticello; Friday and Saturday nights, we'd be at the Chalet at the Pines Hotel. Every summer had its coming-of-age movie-like experiences, which will ever continue to have an impact on my life.

SARI STRICKLER BREUER

Sari and her twin sisters

At 3 p.m. on Fridays, all my friends were making plans for parties, dates and sleepovers. But not me; 3 p.m. on Fridays was when my dad, mom and two older sisters would come to pick me up from school in Brooklyn to start on our 2½-hour journey up the New York State Thruway, aka the Quickway, to South Fallsburg and the Brickman! My friends would always ask me, "Aren't you pissed that you have to go away every weekend and then for the whole summer?" My reply: "Absolutely not. I am going to my happy place!"

As we drove up in the car, I remember the excitement growing as I read the billboards for all the different hotels and restaurants that lie just ahead. The first words I ever read were the names on those signs. And then the countdown of exits to 107 — arrived! The big green-lettered Brickman sign, the security booth in front with the lobby to our left and the big parking lot just outside my home away from home, the Capital Building.

I was too young to experience the *Dirty Dancing* era, but my memories were no less wonderful. The weekend trips were fun, but it is the summers that I remember best. Sunday was both the best and worst day of the week. I would be so excited to sit at the day camp and later the teen-welcoming desk to see who would be arriving. What new best friend would I make, and more importantly, what cute new boys would I be flirting with for the week? But it was also the day I had to say goodbye to the incredible friends I had made over the past seven days.

I went to day camp every day, but before long, I had free range of this entire big "playground": three lobbies, two pools, tennis courts, basketball courts, a softball field, a nightclub, a teen disco, a game room (my favorite was air hockey), a ping-pong room, the coffee shop and so much more. The best time of all was Anniversary Week in August, seven days of special activities and parades culminating in the Kiddie Kamp Karnival, complete with a kissing booth, a dunk-the-staff event and more.

Then, in the blink of an eye, it was Labor Day, time to say goodbye. The tears were real. But then, for a while in the young post-season, there would still be 3 p.m. on Fridays, and we'd be back on the Quickway heading for exit 107.

As I got older and saw the other hotels, I developed an even richer appreciation of the Brickman. It might not have been the biggest or the fanciest, but it was the most beautiful, true country resort in the Catskills. The grove, the riding stables, the best pool in the area and, most importantly, the best staff. It truly was my happy place.

My View from the Mountains

ALLEN SHEINMAN
Brickman day camp counselor, coffee-shop fountain man, 1970–1974

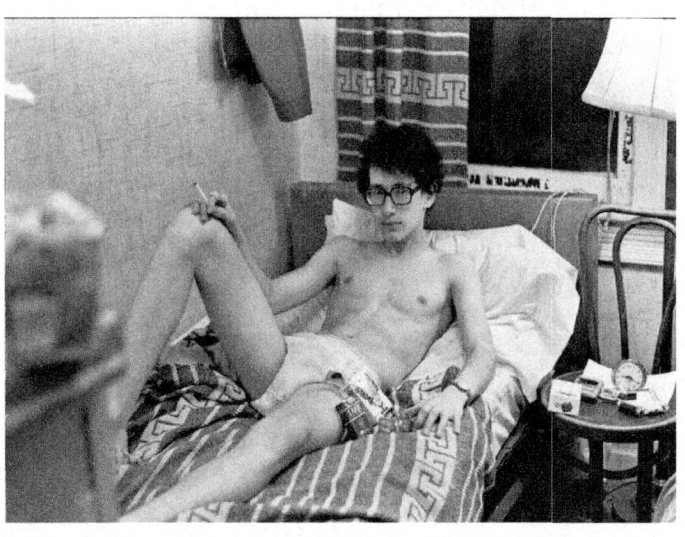

Allen in his room in the Valley Cottage

I spent ages 17-21 at the hotel. I was first made aware of the Brickman when my best friend, Lenny Klein, was lucky enough to start working there at age 14 when his mom was hired to teach folk dancing. I was so jealous! The place seemed so glamorous, there were so many cute girl guests our age. I couldn't wait until I was old enough to join the staff!

So at 17, I lied and said I was 18 and got a job in the day camp, which was the lowest rung on the staff ladder. We put in a full day trying to keep the pre-teens, generally a spoiled and restless lot, occupied. Along with my co-conspirator, Lloyd Schwartz, we tried to get through the long day with minimal effort, using ploys such as art contests where the winner was whomever took the longest to do a picture!

The next four summers I spent in the coffee shop, first under the watch of manager Ira Hammond and then my last two years with Smitty Greenberg. Ira became a surrogate father and good friend for 45 years. He taught me the true way to make an egg cream (milk first, then the seltzer, *then* the syrup). Smitty was a sweet guy and father of my '74 roommate, Rick.

Boy, I look back, amazed at my stamina, the way my hotel friends and I partied out on our off time (all those all-nighters!). But more important was the way I found myself becoming an autonomous person, living on my own for the first time in my life. These were important, formative years for me, and I'm glad I spent them in this unique environment.

HOWARD BELFOR
Coffee-shop counter/grill man, 1968–1972

Howard Belfor, Lloyd Schwartz, Lenny Klein,
Allen Sheinman, early 2000s

Wow, only 54 years ago, a 17-year-old me was driving every week from Avenel, N.J., to South Fallsburg, to his job in the Brickman Coffee Shop. The gig had started on weekends right after Passover that year. My folks had informed me that they were not going to be staying together. While they were pleased about that, I had just been accepted into a college, and they told me they would not be able to offer any financial assistance. So in February 1968, I was penning letters to resorts in Sullivan County to secure a job to pay for school.

Belfor was not a foreign name in the annals of Sullivan County. Until I was seven, we all (including my brother and sister) lived in Woodridge, N.Y., the next town over from Fallsburg. In fact, Dad went to the same school as Ben Posner.

So just before Passover '68, I received a call in which two voices introduced themselves as Murray Posner, owner, and Michael Dern, coffee shop manager. The hunt was on for a counterman. I had just joined my first remote interview.

Two questions clinched the deal. First up: "Do you know how to make an egg cream?" My answer was, "Yes, I do, but which flavor? They are prepared differently to achieve the frothy head." A winner answer. Second question: "Do you know what a bain marie is?" My answer: "Yes, I do, but there are two types — a cold and a hot bain marie, one refrigerated for livestock and the other like a steam table for hot prepared dishes. Oh, by the way, the name is derived from the French." Winner again. (Thanks to Mom for providing this tidbit years earlier when we remodeled our family's luncheonette cooking area.)

Next, I heard, "Can you come up this weekend? When you get here, ask for Rocky Black at the bellhop desk, and he'll assign you a room." Soon after, I discovered Rocky Black wasn't a huge hit man, but a Brooklynite whose real name was Rachmeil Schwartz.

Back then, the minimum driving age in New York was 18, so for three months, until my next birthday, I illegally plied the roads to and from my weekend job. Years later, I learned that my classmates had wondered why I rushed away after school on Fridays. I left for the 120-mile drive directly from school to make sure I got to my post by 6:30 p.m.

I worked each Friday night, Saturday day, and Saturday night until early Sunday morning, leaving at dawn after an exhausting night of penny-point pinball in the rec room. The rest is history. I was the soda jerk they wanted and grew into the short-order chef during the summers from '68 through '72. Due to my habits, I more than once failed to open on time in the mornings. I can still picture Ben staring down from the loading dock behind the kitchen with his hands on his hips. "Trouble getting up? You work nights now." Best time ever.

LEONARD KLEIN
Son of the hotel dance instructor, Lila King;
various staff positions 1967–1971

I began my five-year stint at the Brickman when I was 14. My mom was hired as the folk dance instructor, and the deal was that I came with her, and my dad could come up every weekend. I was skating on thin ice: Murray and Ben had been burned once before by a staff member's kid who had dissed a guest, who in turn made a ruckus and cut their vacation short. This could not happen again, so I was trained for months by my folks to keep my big mouth shut.

Still, Murray and Ben were afraid I'd get into trouble with nothing to do all day, so they decided I would "work" for the head of housekeeping, Mrs. MacGuire, for a few hours each day. I would be paid $2 per hour, and boy, was I proud to go to the payment window and pick up my weekly check, just like all the adult staff. I also earned tips, as I was on call to deliver towels, extra bedding, and catering to any housekeeping needs of the guests. It wasn't until years later that I learned my "pay" was actually taken out of my mom's salary, so *she* was paying me.

In time I graduated to man the pool canteen, where I scored a big success in adding frozen Milky Way bars to the snack repertoire. From there, I began working in the coffee shop behind the counter and then in the kitchen, which gave me the foundation to someday become a cook and then a chef.

Every Sunday, aka check-in day, Marty Gluck, who ran the teen program, would escort me into the dining room for the first dinner and introduce me to all the newly arrived girls. I had a different girlfriend each week. That was great, except for the rare times one of them would return to the hotel later in the summer and find me with a new girl.

This summer life at the hotel was for me the equivalent of going away to college. Once I was old enough to stop rooming with my folks, I roomed with an older, more experienced guy who taught me about the coffee shop and, more importantly, sex, nitrous oxide, hashish and more. I had numerous celebrity encounters, including urinating next to Red Buttons, dog-sitting for Rip Taylor, serving breakfast to Tiny Tim and schmoozing with Totie Fields. Those summers are etched in my memory as some of the best times of my life.

Patti Posner

THE LOARCA FAMILY
JACINTO, VIOLETA, FERNANDO, JULIO, CAESAR, DORA, ALCIRA
1972–1986
(This is part of their eulogy for my dad, Ben Posner)

Jacinto and Violetta Loarca

The Brickman meant so much to all its kitchen workers. The hotel provided so many people, including our family, the opportunity to pull themselves out of poverty. Our father, Jacinto, was in charge of getting some of the kitchen staff at the beginning of each spring. He never had any problems finding people willing to travel to Sullivan County to work at the hotel. In fact, these people anxiously awaited the opening of the hotel each year so they could pay their bills. As the workers arrived, Ben Posner would greet them and ask, "How was your trip?" And then, he would tell them to go to the kitchen and get something to eat. Ben's caring words of welcome meant so much to each of them.

Mom and Dad were Ben's employees, but in his eyes we were family. To us, he was our grandfather. Because of him, my brothers and sisters and I enjoyed a happy childhood. It is because of him that we became successful in the USA, and it is because of him that all of our parents' grandchildren will be spared the pain of poverty. He was the single most influential figure in our lives.

After Ben brought our family to the Brickman following the devastating earthquake that destroyed our home in Guatemala, he gave our parents full-time employment and the rest of us part-time employment to pay for college. He also gave us free housing for 12 years and much more. Our sisters always recall that when they first arrived in the U.S., they had never seen snow. They came without winter clothing, but they were so fascinated by the snow that they kept inching toward the door wanting to go outside and play. Ben ran into his closet, found warm clothing and shoes about six sizes too big, dressed them and watched them play and roll around in the snow.

When our nephew Adam died, Ben called our brother and cried with him over the phone. He talked about when his firstborn died and how he had worked through his grief.

The first day Ben drove us to school, he walked us into the principal's office and made him call the superintendent. I don't know what he told them, but in less than 15 minutes we were all sitting in a classroom attending school. After high school, one brother was devastated that no college would accept him because he could not produce a green card. Because of this, Ben's mission became for us to get our green cards and eventually our citizenship. Thanks to Ben, we are now U.S. citizens.

STEVEN KUNIS
Coffee shop manager, 1966–1967

I served as the coffee shop and lobby bar manager for two years. Until then, I had worked at my dad's luncheonette in South Fallsburg. I started as a grillman during Passover of 1966. Lo and behold, the coffee shop manager at the time had a heart attack. There was now a job opening.

At the end of Passover, I applied for the position of coffee shop manager. I practically begged Ben and Murray for the job. They thought I was too young at 19 years old, but eventually they hired me. They paid me $2,500 for the season, big money in those days. In addition to managing the shop, I managed the lobby smoke shop and was in charge of filling four cigarette machines and keeping Murray and Helen Posner well-supplied with Newports.

The Posners were a wonderful family to work for. They entrusted me with a very responsible position. They instilled confidence in me with their positive management style, a style that I adopted as my own. From Brickman's, it was on to a successful career in the hotel industry. Without Murray and Ben, there would not have been bigger and better things for this local country boy.

BRUCE ELFANT
Waiter, 1975–1986

My time at the Brickman shaped my life. Even after becoming a New York City school teacher, I continued to work at the hotel in the summer (and some off-seasons). I remember every Friday changing into my "black and whites" [black pants, white shirt] in the school bathroom in Brooklyn, putting my students on their school bus, and jumping into my car to drive up to the mountains just in time to greet my guests and offer a choice of chopped liver or gefilte fish to start their Friday dinner (they usually wanted both). I still have my waiter's tray (can I keep it, Patti?)!

The opportunity to work there was like getting your foot into the Goldman Sachs boardroom — you got two meals a day in the summer! The Brickman was the pride of the hotel fleet. We called it "a station with a vacation." Our captain, Solly Gaines (RIP), taught us to be professional, thorough, punctual, respectful and kind. We were all misfits, flunkies, lackeys and pseudo-intellectuals.

Multiculturalism was the order of the day (aside from everything from omelets to latkes). My experience there infused me into a working/cohabitating world of locals from South Fallsburg, illegals from Bogota, gay/straight, black/white, Asian, women/men, young/old and LGBQ (long before it was trendy). I loved and laughed with each of them even as I cut the main line for an order of blintzes.

The escapades are far too many to recount, including the tradition of ingesting Quaaludes during desert to get wasted by the end of the meal, just in time to go out to nearby watering holes like the Old Mill, Bum and Kel's or to go dancing at the Chalet or Down Under in Monticello, or driving to New Paltz after dinner, looking to score and getting back (hopefully) in time to serve breakfast. Or hanging in the rear of the nightclub watching world-famous entertainers and chilling by the pool (back row only; "these lounges are for the paying guests"). Or playing tennis or basketball while gloating as our friends at the other hotels were serving lunch (suckers).

Did I mention I met my future wife, the mother of my children while serving as her busboy?

MARILYN SAUNDERS
Daughter of Bill Rothstein, sax player in Ned Harvey's band; staff singer, 1966

Performing at the day camp

My dad, Billy Rothstein, went to the Brickman Hotel every summer in the 1950s. He was the sax player in the Ned Harvey Orchestra. My mom, brother, sister and I got to spend two glorious weeks there every summer. How I waited and waited for that day. We would leave Brooklyn at 7 a.m. My mom had been up most of the night packing for our trip. We piled into our car and arrived in time for the "late breakfast."

We stayed in the Valley Cottage with my dad. All five of us in one room. I loved the Valley Cottage. I wanted to become a singer, and here I was, living among the musicians. I sat in on rehearsals, which enthralled me. I loved eating in the staff dining room. I grew up on a modest musician's salary. So this was all heaven to me.

Fast forward: I became a singer, and the summer I turned 18, I stayed at the Brickman in the same Valley Cottage and performed one show a week for my room and board. It was a great stepping stone for me on my way to the Broadway stage. I will always cherish the opportunity I was given by the Posner family. How lucky this little girl from Brooklyn was to experience this magical world!

BARRY ADELMAN
Bellhop, 1975–1977

Rocky and Barry

I was New York City born and bred. For me growing up, summers were spent in Northwestern New Jersey near the Pennsylvania border at a family bungalow colony. It was not until I was 20 that I first set foot in the Catskills, when the mountains had a reputation as *the* place to vacation.

Through my older cousin I was introduced to Rocky Black, the head of the bellhops at the Brickman. Hired in the late spring of 1975, I called myself a "luggage engineer." I'd come back for two more summers and work weekends and other holidays, as my upstate New York college was a 90-minute drive away.

How nice it was that the employees felt like family, like part of the hotel experience. We had our own living area, a dorm room that we called the BHQ — Bellhops Quarters. When we were not working (and Murray made it abundantly clear that we needed to behave appropriately), we got to use the facilities such as the pool, tennis courts and even attend the nightclub. It was like being a hotel guest, except we got paid.

I learned things too — how to treat and interact with people, handle problems, how to live up to expectations, how to work hard and how to make a buck. As a bellhop, I checked people in their rooms, for a tip of anywhere near $2 a bag to $5 a bag, or at rare times, no tip at all. We also made money bringing ice to rooms, working the art auction and hosting card games — a big-dollar proposition since the players usually put in money for each hand they played to pay for the bellhop's service of bringing food, drinks and keeping the table clean. I saved thousands of dollars from my job in the summer season and felt like I had a summer vacation as well at a nice resort hotel.

For us bellhops, there was a day shift and night shift. Working nights was great in that you got to play during the day, which meant hanging out at the pool or the coffee shop with other idle staff. For the night shift, you got dressed up: The uniform was a gold vest with "Brickman Hotel" embroidered on it, a white shirt and a clip-on tie. The clip-on upgraded us and transformed the hotel into a Monaco resort, or so I thought. As evening fell, our job would be to close curtains and adjust the lights in the hotel's large lobbies as guests meandered through on their way to the evening's entertainment. My boss, Rocky, would walk through each area like a general, ensuring his bellhops set the proper ambiance.

Along the way, I met some wonderful people who had spent their lives working for the hotel. There was A.D., the maintenance man, a big black guy who was a Korean War veteran and exuded a love of life. He was a bit illiterate, and I helped him with reading and learning words. I took him to see *Star Wars* the year it opened, and he was enthralled.

There was Marcelino, a porter from Spain who was the strongest man I knew and had a heart of gold. There was Joanie, a front-office clerk who always had an uplifting word for everyone every day. There was Abby, Smooth, Ralph, Richie and Steve. The staff of eight bellhops changed over the years, and thanks to social media, I get to stay in touch with some of them. Together we worked hard, played hard and spent a few summers of our youth in a place and in a culture that sadly are long gone. But I got to keep part of it!

It happened in late August of 1975 at an end-of-the-season staff farewell party at a bar in the nearby town of Hurleyville. We met in a loud, boisterous bar with cheap drinks and a ratty pool table. She was a Brickman cocktail waitress from Westchester. She went to college nearby. We talked, flirted and drank. We made a date for the following day, as we both were off. She told me about a waterfall and swimming hole not far in a place called Yagerville. We rendezvoused in the morning and spent the day playing with a rope swing and a natural rock-formed waterslide. I kissed her from behind a waterfall, informing her it was a required custom. That was 47 years ago. We married in 1983, raised two great kids who went on to obtain advanced degrees, sharing our lives with many beloved friends, family and loyal pets.

To this day, we love to share our recollections of the Catskills and the Brickman. You can say that I checked into this memorable, open-hearted hotel, but really never checked out.

RON SUNDICK
Waiter, 1970–1976

Ron (right) with busboy

It was late spring 1970, the end of my junior year in college when Kent State happened, and my university, along with hundreds of others, abruptly closed. Needing a summer job, I got in my car and headed to the Catskills, driving from hotel to hotel. I was interviewed by Murray Posner, who hired me and others in the same situation. I landed first in the staff dining room and soon was a busboy in the main dining room.

I ultimately became a captain in the dining room. During the summer of 1972, I met Robin, the love of my life, who was working in the day camp. We dated all year, worked post-season weekends and returned for summer 1973, when we got engaged and then married before the end of the year. Shelly and Larry Strickler, who had first brought Robin from Brooklyn to work at the hotel, were at our wedding, along with several other Brickman friends.

The Posners were wonderful employers as long as you worked hard. The comradery among the hotel staff, no matter where we worked, was something I'll never forget, and to this day, 52 years later, I'm still in touch with many of them, including Patti Posner, in part due to the friendships and bonds we had while working, but also in large part due to the Posner family, who always showed their appreciation and love of their hotel, guests and staff.

ORLANDO PEREZ
Bartender, 1978–1986

My life at the Brickman was nothing less than extraordinary. It was on a cold March morning in 1978. I was in New York visiting my sister. She mentioned to me that some hotels in upstate New York, the Catskills, were looking for employees. Without any hesitation, I grabbed a newspaper, and there it was. An ad for a job at the Brickman Hotel. I called the employment agency, and they hired me. I was on the bus to Monticello the following day. When I arrived in Monticello, I was so astonished that the owner of the hotel, Ben Posner, was there to pick me up.

Ben introduced me to the other employees and assured me that I would do great. My first job was helping with the opening of the hotel, with the first guests arriving in just a week. I also helped feed the staff, peel onions and wash dishes. When the hotel opened, I became a porter in the bar. Eventually, I was promoted to bartender and then to bar manager. My Hotel Brickman memories remain with me, bringing me such joy.

PETE TWEED
Martial arts instructor

Pete (left) with Johnny Yune

I knew on the day I arrived at the hotel that the rest of my life would change forever. I needed to leave the city. The Bronx wasn't getting any better or safer for me. All I knew was that I would have a job that included room and board. I didn't even know what room and board was. What I knew was limited to martial arts and gymnastics.

My wisdom came from Zen and Tao Te Ching. I had no knowledge about the world or history. When I arrived at the Brickman, I was not aware of what my job would be, and I don't think the Posners did either. They started me in the laundry room, where my duties were to fold towels and sometimes deliver them to a room when a guest would request them.

Although that was fun, that's not where my adventures at the hotel began. As I mentioned, my passion was martial arts and gymnastics. I practiced every morning. I began teaching some of the staff, so I could practice. I didn't know I was being watched. One of the people that was watching me was Ben Posner. He talked to me almost every day, like a grandfather speaking to his grandson. He gave me life advice, told me stories and introduced me to Chinese cookies.

Eventually, I was transferred to the nightclub where I met a lot of entertainers, including Johnny Yune, to whom I taught martial arts. Then, Larry Strickler asked if I was interested in doing a self-defense demonstration. I finally had the chance to do what I was born to do. Entertain people with my talents.

One of the bits I did was put a lit cigarette in a guest's mouth and then put it out while I was blindfolded or had my eyes closed with the Nunchakus, a martial arts weapon consisting of two connected sticks. This was daring, right? Not for me. But definitely for the guest.

I gained popularity with the ladies, but unfortunately, one of the other workers became jealous of the attention I was getting. He actually called the local police department and told them that I had nunchakus, which were banned in New York State. The police came to the hotel and arrested me. I was so nervous. I tried to explain that I only used them for demonstrations and entertainment. The arresting officer suggested I talk to the district attorney because he also was a martial artist.

I'm unsure of what transpired, but they let me go. Later on, I found out that it was Ben Posner who intervened. He told them that if they arrested me, he was going to sue them because they came into his property to make the arrest. I felt so grateful and relieved.

Patti Posner

JESSICA SCHEIN

Jessica and her mom, Ruth Schein

Helen Posner was my aunt. My mother, Ruth, and Helen were sisters. I always was considered part of the Brickman/Posner family. My aunt and uncle had no children, and I developed deep bonds with them, perhaps because I am an only child.

The hotel was my family's second home. Up until the hotel was sold, I visited several times a year. When I was about four, my parents and I moved to a neighborhood in Brooklyn that was undergoing a transition from industrial to high-rise residential. Fire engines and sirens could be heard day and night. The nose from the sirens and fears of nearby fires were sources of anxiety for me. I had trouble falling asleep. But all my fears and anxiety dissipated when we went to the Brickman. I was able to separate the "safe Country" from the "noisy City." The hotel was my safe place.

As a child, I had health issues, and as a result my outside activities were limited during the winter. Since we went to the Brickman in the warmer weather, I could participate in many more activities. I also had several food allergies, but since there were so many options on the menu, my meals were more relaxed. As a result, my overprotective parents were not as concerned about me as they were in the city. The gift of being at the Brickman was independence. I was allowed to do what I wanted. I could choose to go to day camp or not. As a teen, I could hang with the teen group, sit with the bellhops while they supplied the refreshments to the men who were playing poker, go to the coffee shop before the show, play the pinball machines with other kids or just go for a walk around the property.

I didn't have a curfew and often went to the evening shows. Sometimes I brought my friends along. They still remember their time there.

DAVID SHARIN

Miriam Sharin and Larry Strickler at the outdoor pool

Often, I watched my mother lead her dance classes at the outdoor pool patio. She always looked forward to performing with Larry Strickler. My mother, Miriam Sharin, was the resident folk and line dance teacher at the Brickman Hotel from 1976 until 1986. I was ten when we first went to the hotel. I was in the unique position of being considered staff but also got to participate in the many activities the hotel offered. During my first few summers, I spent part of the summer at sleepaway camp and the rest of the time at the hotel. My mom and I (and my dad on weekends) shared a small corner room in the Capital, where many of the staff lived. The floor had shared bathrooms and showers.

As I got older, I joined the teen program. I especially liked this because I got to eat in the main dining room, while my parents ate in the staff dining room. My memories are endless. I formed many friendships that rekindled every summer as many guests returned to vacation at the hotel. My fondest memories include disco dancing in the lounge. playing pinball, ping pong and video games in the game room, playing softball and basketball against other hotels and bungalow colonies, horseback riding, and row boating at Morningside Park. I learned to play tennis on both hard and clay courts. I enjoyed the cocktail parties in the Casino, and saw so many shows in the nightclub with acts including Jackie Mason, Milton Berle, Sal Richards, Mal Z Lawrence and Freddy Roman.

As I got older, I found ways to make some money. Starting with babysitting, I eventually graduated to day camp counselor. Brickman's became my second home and family to me. Nowhere I have gone since has come even close.

JEFFREY ALEXANDER
A Brickman guest

Milton Berle at the Hotel Brickman

My favorite Brickman memory — one year we booked late and we were in a room across from the entrance and next to a room where some of the performers stayed.

One day I was coming to the room and who was entering his room, but Milton Berle. Now, I didn't know who he was, I only knew that he was a big deal. We spoke for a bit, he signed an autograph for me, and when it became clear to him that I didn't know who he was, he said: "I'm going to be on the Love Boat." I told him that The Love Boat was past my bedtime and that my mother wouldn't let me stay up that late. Milton responded, "Maybe she will make an exception."

The next year, we went back to the hotel. My dad checked in while we waited. He came back to us and told us the front desk clerk told him how Milton Berle did this hysterical routine the night before about this rotten kid who didn't know who he was and whose mom wouldn't let him stay up late enough to watch "Love Boat."

Glad I could help you out, Milton.

OMI OMKAR NOAH NADERI

I actually grew up in the ashram that replaced the buildings of the Hotel Brickman, from the late 1980s through the late 2000s. Every year I was there, I always imagined what life was like when it was in its original form as the Hotel Brickman. I would see the buildings — all of which I deeply loved, having had so many priceless memories there — and wondered who was there earlier, what this place meant to those people, and what events took place. I never actually knew it was so beloved by you guys until I saw the Summers at the Brickman Facebook page and out of curiosity I joined. I've been fascinated by many of the old photos, posts and how much nostalgia carries on with this place to this day.

What is most beautiful to me is that this place held such dear memories not just in the version of it that I knew, but that this was always going on. I can see how the joyous energy of the hotel experience permeated the atmosphere in ways that I didn't know during all the years I was there.

In fact, I always wondered—if the ashram was sold, would the people who had the buildings next feel what we felt? The ashram is still there. But my theory that the energy of a place carries on definitely carries sound evidence by all the beautiful shares on this Facebook group!

ACKNOWLEDGEMENTS

Even though I had my share of challenges in my formative years, I look back at my time at the hotel with deep gratitude for the experiences it provided. The world came to me, in the guise of our guests and staff, providing me with wonderful relationships and unusual experiences.

I worked on this book for many years. When I was in my early 20s, my lifetime friend, David Gold, suggested that I write a memoir, but I was too young at the time, my story was still developing. It was only when I turned 50 that I felt ready to look back on my life. Over the ensuing years, I wrote on and off, collecting memories and perspective, mainly focusing on my personal life. In 2014, when I moved to Weaverville, North Carolina, and was living in a small town in the Blue Ridge Mountains, life felt akin to growing up in the Catskills. And the rest of my memoir began to flow.

My husband, an artist, helped me find the confidence to reach out to Allen Sheinman, a dear friend and editor who worked at the hotel in the coffee shop in the 1970s. We were unexpectedly reunited about 30 years ago and have remained good friends ever since. Trusting my story to Allen was scary at first, but he was welcoming and encouraging — and his own deep connection to his Catskills experience gave us a rich field of common ground.

Allen worked his artistry to sculpt my manuscript into a memoir. I will be forever grateful to him for helping me become a better writer. He has been there for me all through this process, from the prologue to the final approved book cover.

I asked several friends to read my memoir when the first draft was complete. Their feedback was invaluable.

Barbara Francois was my first reader, but she was much more than that. We met several years ago in a writing group and immediately became dear friends and writing companions. After each chapter felt complete, off it went to Barbara for her comments, compliments and critiques. Without her help and support, I am not sure I could have completed my book.

Thank you to Larry and Shelly Strickler for all your years of friendship (58 years and counting), for all the fun times we had while

Larry was director of activities at the Hotel Brickman and for all your encouragement and interest in my story.

To their daughter and author, Marcy Strickler McCreary, thank you for your suggestions that helped make my book what it is.

To my BFF, Debby Cavanagh, thank you. Debby knew me when I was married to Michael, and I wanted her to look clearly at the sections of the book that dealt with that marriage. Her observations were invaluable, as is her friendship.

To Rita Brickman Domnitz. When our family reunited, Rita was the first cousin I met, and to this day we are close friends as well as family. I asked her to read my memoir because I wanted to make sure that the information about our Brickman family was correct. But I also wanted to share my story with a member of my family. When Rita said she enjoyed reading my book, I could feel our ancestors smiling.

After my friends gave me their critiques and compliments, it was time to tell David Gold that my book was finally finished. Every once in a while, David would ask me how it was coming along. And when I finally told him the memoir was complete, he said he would like to read it. I was thrilled. When he told me he liked my work, I felt a wave of confidence embrace me. Then he went further; his insights, tough questions and knowledge of local history were invaluable. When I was having trouble preparing the manuscript for publication, David once again stepped up and formatted the book. He was there from the very beginning to the very end of this project.

To Saul Rothenberg. Thank you for allowing me to use your photograph of the Catskill mountains on the cover of the book.

To all the Other Voices, thank you for sharing your stories of your time at the Brickman.

And finally to Yossi Daboosh, my husband. Thank you for all your encouragement, particularly for imparting your wisdom on welcoming other artists to critique your art, which helped me to appreciate the evaluation of my work by others.

And to all the people who had the time of their lives in the Catskills, and particularly at the Hotel Brickman, thank you.

Printed in Great Britain
by Amazon